4/10

LIT

D0773013

The Merchant of Venice

SARA SCHUPACK
INTRODUCTION BY JOSEPH SOBRAN

mc **Marshall Cavendish**
Benchmark
New York

Series consultant: Richard Larkin

Marshall Cavendish
99 White Plains Road
Tarrytown, New York 10591
www.marshallcavendish.us

Library of Congress Cataloging-in-Publication Data
Schupack, Sara.
The merchant of Venice / by Sara Schupack.
p. cm. — (Shakespeare explained)
Summary: "A literary analysis of Shakespeare's play The Merchant of
Venice. Includes information on the history and culture of Elizabethan
England"—Provided by publisher.
Includes bibliographical references and index.
ISBN 978-0-7614-3421-4
1. Shakespeare, William, 1564–1616. Merchant of Venice—Juvenile
literature. I. Title.
PR2825.S36 2009
822.3'3—dc22
2009003166

Photo research by: Linda Sykes
Nigel Norrington/ArenaPAL/Topfoto/The Image Works: cover; istockphoto: 1; Neven Mendrila/
Shutterstock: 3; Raciro/istockphoto: 4; Art Parts RF: 6, 8, 13, 24, 25; ©Nik Wheeler/Corbis:
11; Portraitgalerie, Schloss Ambras, Innsbruck, Austria/Erich Lessing/Art Resource, NY: 18;
AA World Travel Library/Alamy: 20; ©Hideo Kurihara/Alamy: 22; Corbis/Sygma: 27; Andrew Fox/
Corbis: 30; City of Westminster Archive Centre, London/Bridgeman Art Library: 37; Royal National
Theatre: 43; ©Sony Pictures Classics/The Everett Collection: 97; National Pictures/Topfoto/
The Image Works: 47; Mary Evans Picture Library/The Everett Collection: 50; Nigel Norrington/
ArenaPAL/Topfoto/The Image Works: 54, 77, 83; Yale Center for British Art, Paul Mellon Fund/
Bridgeman Art Library: 58; Private Collection/Bridgeman Art Library: 64; Sony Pictures Classics
The Kobal Collection: 67; The Everett Collection: 79.

Editor: Deborah Grahame
Publisher: Michelle Bisson
Art Director: Anahid Hamparian
Series Design: Kay Petronio

Printed in Malaysia
135642

Contents

Shakespeare and His World

WILLIAM SHAKESPEARE, OFTEN NICKNAMED "THE BARD," IS, BEYOND ANY COMPARISON, THE MOST TOWERING NAME IN ENGLISH LITERATURE. MANY CONSIDER HIS PLAYS THE GREATEST EVER WRITTEN. HE STANDS OUT EVEN AMONG GENIUSES.

Yet the Bard is also closer to our hearts than lesser writers, and his tremendous reputation should neither intimidate us nor prevent us from enjoying the simple delights he offers in such abundance. It is as if he had written for each of us personally. As he himself put it, "One touch of nature makes the whole world kin."

Such tragedies as *Hamlet*, *Romeo and Juliet*, and *Macbeth* are world-famous, still performed on stage and in films. These and others have also been adapted for radio, television, opera, ballet, pantomime, novels, comic books, and other media. Two of the best ways to become familiar with them are to watch some of the many fine movies that have been made of them and to listen to recordings of them by some of the world's great actors.

Even Shakespeare's individual characters have a life of their own, like real historical figures. Hamlet is still regarded as the most challenging role ever written for an actor. Roughly as many whole books have been written about Hamlet, an imaginary character, as about actual historical figures such as Abraham Lincoln and Napoleon Bonaparte.

Shakespeare created an amazing variety of vivid characters. One of Shakespeare's most peculiar traits was that he loved his characters so much—even some of his villains and secondary or comic characters—that at times he let them run away with the play, stealing attention from his heroes and heroines.

So in *A Midsummer Night's Dream* audiences remember the absurd and lovable fool Bottom the Weaver better than the lovers who are the main characters. Romeo's friend Mercutio is more fiery and witty than Romeo himself; legend claims that Shakespeare said he had to kill Mercutio or Mercutio would have killed the play.

Shakespeare also wrote dozens of comedies and historical plays, as well as nondramatic poems. Although his tragedies are now regarded as his greatest works, he freely mixed them with comedy and history. And his sonnets are among the supreme love poems in the English language.

It is Shakespeare's mastery of the English language that keeps his words familiar to us today. Every literate person knows dramatic lines such as "Wherefore art thou Romeo?"; "My kingdom for a horse!"; "To be or not to be: that is the question"; "Friends, Romans, countrymen, lend me your ears"; and "What fools these mortals be!" Shakespeare's sonnets are noted for their sweetness: "Shall I compare thee to a summer's day?"

IN THE TWINKLING OF AN EYE.

SHAKESPEARE'S LANGUAGE

WITHOUT A DOUBT, SHAKESPEARE WAS THE GREATEST MASTER OF THE ENGLISH LANGUAGE WHO EVER LIVED. BUT JUST WHAT DOES THAT MEAN?

Shakespeare's vocabulary was huge, full of references to the Bible as well as Greek and Roman mythology. Yet his most brilliant phrases often combine very simple and familiar words:

"WHAT'S IN A NAME? THAT WHICH WE CALL A ROSE BY ANY OTHER NAME WOULD SMELL AS SWEET."

He has delighted countless millions of readers. And we know him only through his language. He has shaped modern English far more than any other writer.

Or, to put it in more personal terms, you probably quote his words several times every day without realizing it, even if you have never suspected that Shakespeare could be a source of pleasure to you.

So why do so many English-speaking readers find his language so difficult? It is our language, too, but it has changed so much that it is no longer quite the same language—nor a completely different one, either.

Shakespeare's English and ours overlap without being identical. He would have some difficulty understanding us, too! Many of our everyday words and phrases would baffle him.

Shakespeare, for example, would not know what we meant by a *car,* a *radio,* a *movie,* a *television,* a *computer,* or a *sitcom,* since these things did not even exist in his time. Our old-fashioned term *railroad train* would be unimaginable to him, far in the distant future. We would have to explain to him (if we could) what *nuclear weapons, electricity,* and *democracy* are. He would also be a little puzzled by common expressions such as *high-tech, feel the heat, approval ratings, war criminal, judgmental,* and *whoopie cushion.*

So how can we call him "the greatest master of the English language"? It might seem as if he barely spoke English at all! (He would, however, recognize much of our dirty slang, even if he pronounced it slightly differently. His plays also contain many racial insults to Jews, Africans, Italians, Irish, and others. Today he would be called "insensitive.")

Many of the words of Shakespeare's time have become archaic. Words like *thou, thee, thy, thyself,* and *thine,* which were among the most common words in the language in Shakespeare's day, have all but disappeared today. We simply say *you* for both singular and plural, formal and familiar. Most other modern languages have kept their *thou.*

Sometimes the same words now have different meanings. We are apt to be misled by such simple, familiar words as *kind, wonderful, waste, just,* and *dear,* which he often uses in ways that differ from our usage.

Shakespeare also doesn't always use the words we expect to hear, the words that we ourselves would naturally use. When we might automatically say, "I beg your pardon" or just "Sorry," he might say, "I cry you mercy."

Often a glossary and footnotes will solve all three of these problems for us. But it is most important to bear in mind that Shakespeare was often hard for his first audiences to understand. Even in his own time his rich language was challenging. And this was deliberate. Shakespeare was inventing his own kind of English. It remains unique today.

A child doesn't learn to talk by using a dictionary. Children learn first by sheer immersion. We teach babies by pointing at things and saying their names. Yet the toddler always learns faster than we can teach! Even as babies we are geniuses. Dictionaries can help us later, when we already speak and read the language well (and learn more slowly).

So the best way to learn Shakespeare is not to depend on the footnotes and glossary too much, but instead to be like a baby: just get into the flow of the language. Go to performances of the plays or watch movies of them.

THE LANGUAGE HAS A MAGICAL WAY OF TEACHING ITSELF, IF WE LET IT. THERE IS NO REASON TO FEEL STUPID OR FRUSTRATED WHEN IT DOESN'T COME EASILY.

Hundreds of phrases have entered the English language from *Hamlet* alone, including "to hold, as t'were, the mirror up to nature"; "murder most foul"; "the thousand natural shocks that flesh is heir to"; "flaming youth"; "a countenance more in sorrow than in anger"; "the play's the thing"; "neither a borrower nor a lender be"; "in my mind's eye"; "something is rotten in the state of Denmark"; "alas, poor Yorick"; and "the lady doth protest too much, methinks."

From other plays we get the phrases "star-crossed lovers"; "what's in a name?"; "we have scotched the snake, not killed it"; "one fell swoop"; "it was Greek to me;" "I come to bury Caesar, not to praise him"; and "the most unkindest cut of all"—all these are among our household words. In fact, Shakespeare even gave us the expression "household words." No wonder his contemporaries marveled at his "fine filed phrase" and swooned at the "mellifluous and honey-tongued Shakespeare."

Shakespeare's words seem to combine music, magic, wisdom, and humor:

"THE COURSE OF TRUE LOVE NEVER DID RUN SMOOTH."

"HE JESTS AT SCARS THAT NEVER FELT A WOUND."

"THE FAULT, DEAR BRUTUS, IS NOT IN OUR STARS,
BUT IN OURSELVES, THAT WE ARE UNDERLINGS."

"COWARDS DIE MANY TIMES BEFORE THEIR DEATHS;
THE VALIANT NEVER TASTE OF DEATH BUT ONCE."

"NOT THAT I LOVED CAESAR LESS, BUT
THAT I LOVED ROME MORE."

"THERE ARE MORE THINGS IN HEAVEN AND EARTH,
HORATIO, THAN ARE DREAMT OF IN YOUR PHILOSOPHY."

"BREVITY IS THE SOUL OF WIT."

"THERE'S A DIVINITY THAT SHAPES OUR ENDS,
ROUGH-HEW THEM HOW WE WILL."

Four centuries after Shakespeare lived, to speak English is to quote him. His huge vocabulary and linguistic fertility are still astonishing. He has had a powerful effect on all of us, whether we realize it or not. We may wonder how it is even possible for a single human being to say so many memorable things.

Only the King James translation of the Bible, perhaps, has had a more profound and pervasive influence on the English language than Shakespeare. And, of course, the Bible was written by many authors over many centuries, and the King James translation, published in 1611, was the combined effort of many scholars.

EARLY LIFE

So who, exactly, was Shakespeare? Mystery surrounds his life, largely because few records were kept during his time. Some people have even doubted his identity, arguing that the real author of Shakespeare's plays must have been a man of superior formal education and wide experience. In a sense such doubts are a natural and understandable reaction to his rare, almost miraculous powers of expression, but some people feel that the doubts themselves show a lack of respect for the supremely human poet.

Most scholars agree that Shakespeare was born in the town of Stratford-upon-Avon in the county of Warwickshire, England, in April 1564. He was baptized, according to local church records, Gulielmus (William) Shakspere (the name was spelled in several different ways) on April 26 of that year. He was one of several children, most of whom died young.

His father, John Shakespeare (or Shakspere), was a glove maker and, at times, a town official. He was often in debt or being fined for unknown delinquencies, perhaps failure to attend church regularly. It is suspected that John was a "recusant" (secret and illegal) Catholic, but there is no proof. Many

SHAKESPEARE'S CHILDHOOD HOME IS CARED FOR BY AN INDEPENDENT CHARITY, THE SHAKESPEARE BIRTHPLACE TRUST, IN STRATFORD-UPON-AVON, WARWICKSHIRE, ENGLAND.

scholars have found Catholic tendencies in Shakespeare's plays, but whether Shakespeare was Catholic or not we can only guess.

At the time of Shakespeare's birth, England was torn by religious controversy and persecution. The country had left the Roman Catholic Church during the reign of King Henry VIII, who had died in 1547. Two of Henry's children, Edward and Mary, ruled after his death. When his daughter Elizabeth I became queen in 1558, she upheld his claim that the monarch of England was also head of the English Church.

Did William attend the local grammar school? He was probably entitled to, given his father's prominence in Stratford, but again, we face a frustrating absence of proof, and many people of the time learned to read very well without schooling. If he went to the town school, he would also have learned the rudiments of Latin.

We know very little about the first half of William's life. In 1582, when he was eighteen, he married Anne Hathaway, eight years his senior. Their first daughter, Susanna, was born six months later. The following year they had twins, Hamnet and Judith.

At this point William disappears from the records again. By the early 1590s we find "William Shakespeare" in London, a member of the city's leading acting company, called the Lord Chamberlain's Men. Many of Shakespeare's greatest roles, we are told, were first performed by the company's star, Richard Burbage.

Curiously, the first work published under (and identified with) Shakespeare's name was not a play but a long erotic poem, *Venus and Adonis*, in 1593. It was dedicated to the young Earl of Southampton, Henry Wriothesley.

Venus and Adonis was a spectacular success, and Shakespeare was immediately hailed as a major poet. In 1594 he dedicated a longer, more serious poem to Southampton, *The Rape of Lucrece*. It was another hit, and for many years, these two poems were considered Shakespeare's greatest works, despite the popularity of his plays.

"IT IS A WISE FATHER THAT KNOWS HIS OWN CHILD."

SHAKESPEARE ON FILM: A SAMPLER

TODAY MOVIES, NOT LIVE PLAYS, ARE THE MORE POPULAR ART FORM. FORTUNATELY MOST OF SHAKESPEARE'S PLAYS HAVE BEEN FILMED, AND THE BEST OF THESE MOVIES OFFER AN EXCELLENT WAY TO MAKE THE BARD'S ACQUAINTANCE. RECENTLY, KENNETH BRANAGH HAS BECOME A RESPECTED CONVERTER OF SHAKESPEARE'S PLAYS INTO FILM.

Hamlet

Hamlet, Shakespeare's most famous play, has been well filmed several times. In 1948 Laurence Olivier won three Academy Awards—for best picture, best actor, and best director—for his version of the play. The film allowed him to show some of the magnetism that made him famous on the stage. Nobody spoke Shakespeare's lines more thrillingly.

The young Derek Jacobi played Hamlet in a 1980 BBC production of the play, with Patrick Stewart (now best known for *Star Trek, the Next Generation*) as the guilty king. Jacobi, like Olivier, has a gift for speaking the lines freshly; he never seems to be merely reciting the famous and familiar words. But whereas Olivier has animal passion, Jacobi is more intellectual. It is fascinating to compare the ways these two outstanding actors play Shakespeare's most complex character.

Franco Zeffirelli's 1990 *Hamlet*, starring Mel Gibson, is fascinating in a different way. Gibson, of course, is best known as an action hero, and he is not well suited to this supremely witty and introspective role, but Zeffirelli cuts the text drastically, and the result turns *Hamlet* into something that few people would have expected: a short, swift-moving action movie. Several of the other characters are brilliantly played.

Henry IV, Part One

The 1979 BBC Shakespeare series production does a commendable job in this straightforward approach to the play. Battle scenes are effective despite obvious restrictions in an indoor studio setting. Anthony Quayle gives jovial Falstaff a darker edge, and Tim Pigott-Smith's Hotspur is buoyed by some humor. Jon Finch plays King Henry IV with noble authority, and David Gwillim gives Hal a surprisingly successful transformation from boy prince to heir apparent.

Julius Caesar

No really good movie of *Julius Caesar* exists, but the 1953 film, with Marlon Brando as Mark Antony, will do. James Mason is a thoughtful Brutus, and John Gielgud, then ranked with Laurence Olivier among the greatest Shakespearean actors, plays the villainous Cassius. The film is rather dull, and Brando is out of place in a Roman toga, but it is still worth viewing.

Macbeth

Roman Polanski is best known as a director of thrillers and horror films, so it may seem natural that he should have done his 1971 *The Tragedy of Macbeth* as an often-gruesome slasher flick. But this is also one of the most vigorous of all Shakespeare films. Macbeth and his wife are played by Jon Finch and Francesca Annis, neither known for playing Shakespeare, but they are young and attractive in roles that are usually given to older actors, which gives the story a fresh flavor.

The Merchant of Venice

Once again the matchless Sir Laurence Olivier delivers a great performance as Shylock with his wife Joan Plowright as Portia in the 1974 TV film, adapted from the 1970 National Theater (of Britain) production. A 1980 BBC offering features Warren Mitchell as Shylock and Gemma Jones as Portia, with John Rhys-Davies as Salerio. The most recent production, starring Al Pacino as Shylock, Jeremy Irons as Antonio, and Joseph Fiennes as Bassanio, was filmed in Venice and released in 2004.

A Midsummer Night's Dream

Because of the prestige of his tragedies, we tend to forget how many comedies Shakespeare wrote—nearly twice the number of tragedies. Of these perhaps the most popular has always been the enchanting, atmospheric, and very silly masterpiece *A Midsummer Night's Dream*.

In more recent times several films have been made of *A Midsummer Night's Dream*. Among the more notable have been Max Reinhardt's 1935 black-and-white version, with Mickey Rooney (then a child star) as Puck.

Of the several film versions, the one starring Kevin Kline as Bottom and Stanley Tucci as Puck, made in 1999 with nineteenth-century costumes and directed by Michael Hoffman, ranks among the finest, and is surely one of the most sumptuous to watch.

Othello

Orson Welles did a budget European version in 1952, now available as a restored DVD. Laurence Olivier's 1965 film performance is predictably remarkable, though it has been said that he would only approach the part by honoring, even emulating, Paul Robeson's definitive interpretation that ran on Broadway in 1943. (Robeson was the first black actor to play Othello, the Moor of Venice, and he did so to critical acclaim, though sadly his performance was never filmed.) Maggie Smith plays a formidable Desdemona opposite Olivier, and her youth and energy will surprise younger audiences who know her only from the Harry Potter films. Laurence Fishburne brilliantly portrayed Othello in the 1995 film, costarring with Kenneth Branagh as a surprisingly human Iago, though Irène Jacob's Desdemona was disappointingly weak.

Romeo and Juliet

This, the world's most famous love story, has been filmed many times, twice very successfully over the last generation. Franco Zeffirelli directed a hit version in 1968 with Leonard Whiting and the rapturously pretty Olivia Hussey, set in Renaissance Italy. Baz Luhrmann made a much more contemporary version, with a loud rock score, starring Leonardo Di Caprio and Claire Danes, in 1996.

It seems safe to say that Shakespeare would have preferred Zeffirelli's movie, with its superior acting and rich, romantic, sun-drenched Italian scenery.

The Tempest

A 1960 Hallmark Hall of Fame production featured Maurice Evans as Prospero, Lee Remick as Miranda, Roddy McDowall as Ariel, and Richard Burton as Caliban. The special effects are primitive and the costumes are ludicrous, but it moves along at a fast pace. Another TV version aired in 1998 and was nominated for a Golden Globe. Peter Fonda played Gideon Prosper, and Katherine Heigl played his daughter Miranda Prosper. Sci-Fi fans may already know that the classic 1956 film *Forbidden Planet* is modeled on themes and characters from the play.

Twelfth Night

Trevor Nunn adapted the play for the 1996 film he also directed in a rapturous Edwardian setting, with big names like Helena Bonham Carter, Richard E. Grant, Imogen Stubbs, and Ben Kingsley as Feste. A 2003 film set in modern Britain provides an interesting multicultural experience; it features an Anglo-Indian cast with Parminder Nagra (*Bend It Like Beckham*) playing Viola. For the truly intrepid, a twelve-minute silent film made in 1910 does a fine job of capturing the play through visual gags and over-the-top gesturing.

THESE FILMS HAVE BEEN SELECTED FOR SEVERAL QUALITIES: APPEAL AND ACCESSIBILITY TO MODERN AUDIENCES, EXCELLENCE IN ACTING, PACING, VISUAL BEAUTY, AND, OF COURSE, FIDELITY TO SHAKESPEARE. THEY ARE THE MOTION PICTURES WE JUDGE MOST LIKELY TO HELP STUDENTS UNDERSTAND THE SOURCE OF THE BARD'S LASTING POWER.

SHAKESPEARE'S THEATER

Today we sometimes speak of "live entertainment." In Shakespeare's day, of course, all entertainment was live, because recordings, films, television, and radio did not yet exist. Even printed books were a novelty.

In fact, most communication in those days was difficult. Transportation was not only difficult but slow, chiefly by horse and boat. Most people were illiterate peasants who lived on farms that they seldom left; cities grew up along waterways and were subject to frequent plagues that could wipe out much of the population within weeks.

Money—in coin form, not paper—was scarce and hardly existed outside the cities. By today's standards, even the rich were poor. Life was precarious. Most children died young, and famine or disease might kill anyone at any time. Everyone was familiar with death. Starvation was not rare or remote, as it is to most of us today. Medical care was poor and might kill as many people as it healed.

This was the grim background of Shakespeare's theater during the reign of Queen Elizabeth I, who ruled from 1558 until her death in 1603. During that period England was also torn by religious conflict, often violent, among Roman Catholics who were

ELIZABETH I, A GREAT PATRON OF POETRY AND THE THEATER, WROTE SONNETS AND TRANSLATED CLASSIC WORKS.

loyal to the Pope, adherents of the Church of England who were loyal to the queen, and the Puritans who would take over the country in the revolution of 1642.

Under these conditions, most forms of entertainment were luxuries that were out of most people's reach. The only way to hear music was to be in the actual physical presence of singers or musicians with their instruments, which were primitive by our standards.

One brutal form of entertainment, popular in London, was bear-baiting. A bear was blinded and chained to a stake, where fierce dogs called mastiffs were turned loose to tear him apart. The theaters had to compete with the bear gardens, as they were called, for spectators.

The Puritans, or radical Protestants, objected to bear-baiting and tried to ban it. Despite their modern reputation, the Puritans were anything but conservative. Conservative people, attached to old customs, hated them. They seemed to upset everything. (Many of America's first settlers, such as the Pilgrims who came over on the *Mayflower*, were dissidents who were fleeing the Church of England.)

Plays were extremely popular, but they were primitive, too. They had to be performed outdoors in the afternoon because of the lack of indoor lighting. Often the "theater" was only an enclosed courtyard. Probably the versions of Shakespeare's plays that we know today were not used in full, but shortened to about two hours for actual performance.

But eventually more regular theaters were built, featuring a raised stage extending into the audience. Poorer spectators (illiterate "groundlings") stood on the ground around it, at times exposed to rain and snow. Wealthier people sat in raised tiers above. Aside from some costumes, there were few props or special effects and almost no scenery. Much had to be imagined: Whole battles might be represented by a few actors with swords. Thunder might be simulated by rattling a sheet of tin offstage.

The plays were far from realistic and, under the conditions of the time, could hardly try to be. Above the rear of the main stage was a small balcony. (It was this balcony from which Juliet spoke to Romeo.) Ghosts and witches might appear by entering through a trapdoor in the stage floor.

Unlike the modern theater, Shakespeare's Globe Theater—he describes it as "this wooden O"—had no curtain separating the stage from the audience. This allowed intimacy between the players and the spectators.

THE RECONSTRUCTED GLOBE THEATER WAS COMPLETED IN 1997 AND IS LOCATED IN LONDON, JUST 200 YARDS (183 METERS) FROM THE SITE OF THE ORIGINAL.

THE DEVIL CAN CITE SCRIPTURE FOR HIS PURPOSE.

The spectators probably reacted rowdily to the play, not listening in reverent silence. After all, they had come to have fun! And few of them were scholars. Again, a play had to amuse people who could not read.

The lines of plays were written and spoken in prose or, more often, in a form of verse called iambic pentameter (ten syllables with five stresses per line). There was no attempt at modern realism. Only males were allowed on the stage, so some of the greatest women's roles ever written had to be played by boys or men. (The same is true, by the way, of the ancient Greek theater.)

Actors had to be versatile, skilled not only in acting, but also in fencing, singing, dancing, and acrobatics. Within its limitations, the theater offered a considerable variety of spectacles.

Plays were big business, not yet regarded as high art, sponsored by important and powerful people (the queen loved them as much as the groundlings did). The London acting companies also toured and performed in the provinces. When plagues struck London, the government might order the theaters to be closed to prevent the spread of disease among crowds. (They remained empty for nearly two years from 1593 to 1594.)

As the theater became more popular, the Puritans grew as hostile to it as they were to bear-baiting. Plays, like books, were censored by the government, and the Puritans fought to increase restrictions, eventually banning any mention of God and other sacred topics on the stage.

In 1642 the Puritans shut down all the theaters in London, and in 1644 they had the Globe demolished. The theaters remained closed until Charles's son King Charles II was restored to the throne in 1660 and the hated Puritans were finally vanquished.

But, by then, the tradition of Shakespeare's theater had been fatally interrupted. His plays remained popular, but they were often rewritten by inferior dramatists and it was many years before they were performed (again) as he had originally written them.

THE ROYAL SHAKESPEARE THEATER, IN STRATFORD-UPON-AVON, WAS CLOSED IN 2007. A NEWLY DESIGNED INTERIOR WITH A 1,000-SEAT AUDITORIUM WILL BE COMPLETED IN 2010.

Today, of course, the plays are performed both in theaters and in films, sometimes in costumes of the period (ancient Rome for *Julius Caesar*, medieval England for *Henry V*), sometimes in modern dress (*Richard III* has recently been reset in England in the 1930s).

PLAYS

In the England of Queen Elizabeth I, plays were enjoyed by all classes of people, but they were not yet respected as a serious form of art.

Shakespeare's plays began to appear in print in individual, or "quarto," editions in 1594, but none of these bore his name until 1598. Although his tragedies are now ranked as his supreme achievements, his name was first associated with comedies and with plays about English history.

The dates of Shakespeare's plays are notoriously hard to determine. Few performances of them were documented; some were not printed until decades after they first appeared on the stage. Mainstream scholars generally place most of the comedies and histories in the 1590s, admitting that this time frame is no more than a widely accepted estimate.

The three parts of *King Henry VI*, culminating in a fourth part, *Richard III*, deal with the long and complex dynastic struggle or civil wars known as the Wars of the Roses (1455–1487), one of England's most turbulent periods. Today it is not easy to follow the plots of these plays.

It may seem strange to us that a young playwright should have written such demanding works early in his career, but they were evidently very popular with the Elizabethan public. Of the four, only *Richard III*, with its wonderfully villainous starring role, is still often performed.

Even today, one of Shakespeare's early comedies, *The Taming of the Shrew*, remains a crowd-pleaser. (It has enjoyed success in a 1999 film adaptation, *10 Things I Hate About You*, with Heath Ledger and Julia Stiles.)

THE "REAL" SHAKESPEARE

AROUND 1850 DOUBTS STARTED TO SURFACE ABOUT WHO HAD ACTUALLY WRITTEN SHAKESPEARE'S PLAYS, CHIEFLY BECAUSE MANY OTHER AUTHORS, SUCH AS MARK TWAIN, THOUGHT THE PLAYS' AUTHOR WAS TOO WELL EDUCATED AND KNOWLEDGEABLE TO HAVE BEEN THE MODESTLY SCHOOLED MAN FROM STRATFORD.

Who, then, was the real author? Many answers have been given, but the three leading candidates are Francis Bacon, Christopher Marlowe, and Edward de Vere, Earl of Oxford.

Francis Bacon (1561-1626)

Bacon was a distinguished lawyer, scientist, philosopher, and essayist. Many considered him one of the great geniuses of his time, capable of any literary achievement, though he wrote little poetry and, as far as we know, no dramas. When people began to suspect that "Shakespeare" was only a pen name, he seemed like a natural candidate. But his writing style was vastly different from the style of the plays.

Christopher Marlowe (1564–1593)

Marlowe wrote several excellent tragedies in a style much like that of the Shakespeare tragedies, though without the comic blend. But he was reportedly killed in a mysterious incident in 1593, before most of the Bard's plays existed. Could his death have been faked? Is it possible that he lived on for decades in hiding, writing under a pen name? This is what his advocates contend.

Edward de Vere, Earl of Oxford (1550–1604)

Oxford is now the most popular and plausible alternative to the lad from Stratford. He had a high reputation as a poet and playwright in his day, but his life was full of scandal. That controversial life seems to match what the poet says about himself in the sonnets, as well as many events in the plays (especially *Hamlet*). However, he died in 1604, and most scholars believe this rules him out as the author of plays that were published after that date.

THE GREAT MAJORITY OF EXPERTS REJECT THESE AND ALL OTHER ALTERNATIVE CANDIDATES, STICKING WITH THE TRADITIONAL VIEW, AFFIRMED IN THE 1623 FIRST FOLIO OF THE PLAYS, THAT THE AUTHOR WAS THE MAN FROM STRATFORD. THAT REMAINS THE SAFEST POSITION TO TAKE, UNLESS STARTLING NEW EVIDENCE TURNS UP, WHICH, AT THIS LATE DATE, SEEMS HIGHLY UNLIKELY.

The story is simple: The enterprising Petruchio resolves to marry a rich young woman, Katherina Minola, for her wealth, despite her reputation for having a bad temper. Nothing she does can discourage this dauntless suitor, and the play ends with Kate becoming a submissive wife. It is all the funnier for being unbelievable.

With *Romeo and Juliet* the Bard created his first enduring triumph. This tragedy of "star-crossed lovers" from feuding families is known around the world. Even people with only the vaguest knowledge of Shakespeare are often aware of this universally beloved story. It has inspired countless similar stories and adaptations, such as the hit musical *West Side Story*.

By the mid-1590s Shakespeare was successful and prosperous, a partner in the Lord Chamberlain's Men. He was rich enough to buy New Place, one of the largest houses in his hometown of Stratford.

Yet, at the peak of his good fortune, came the worst sorrow of his life: Hamnet, his only son, died in August 1596 at the age of eleven, leaving nobody to carry on his family name, which was to die out with his two daughters.

Our only evidence of his son's death is a single line in the parish burial register. As far as we know, this crushing loss left no mark on Shakespeare's work. As far as his creative life shows, it was as if nothing had happened. His silence about his grief may be the greatest puzzle of his mysterious life, although, as we shall see, others remain.

During this period, according to traditional dating (even if it must be somewhat hypothetical), came the torrent of Shakespeare's mightiest works. Among these was another quartet of English history plays, this one centering on the legendary King Henry IV, including *Richard II* and the two parts of *Henry IV*.

Then came a series of wonderful romantic comedies: *Much Ado About Nothing*, *As You Like It*, and *Twelfth Night*.

ACTOR JOSEPH FIENNES PORTRAYED THE BARD IN THE 1998 FILM *SHAKESPEARE IN LOVE,* DIRECTED BY JOHN MADDEN.

In 1598 the clergyman Francis Meres, as part of a larger work, hailed Shakespeare as the English Ovid, supreme in love poetry as well as drama. "The Muses would speak with Shakespeare's fine filed phrase," Meres wrote, "if they would speak English." He added praise of Shakespeare's "sugared sonnets among his private friends." It is tantalizing; Meres seems to know something of the poet's personal life, but he gives us no hard information. No wonder biographers are frustrated.

Next the Bard returned gloriously to tragedy with *Julius Caesar.* In the play Caesar has returned to Rome in great popularity after his military triumphs. Brutus and several other leading senators, suspecting that Caesar means to make himself king, plot to assassinate him. Midway through the play, after the assassination, comes one of Shakespeare's most famous scenes. Brutus speaks at Caesar's funeral. But then Caesar's friend Mark Antony delivers a powerful attack on the conspirators, inciting the mob to fury. Brutus and the others, forced to flee Rome, die in the ensuing civil war. In the end the spirit of Caesar wins after all. If Shakespeare had written nothing after *Julius Caesar*, he would still have been remembered as one of the greatest playwrights of all time. But his supreme works were still to come.

Only Shakespeare could have surpassed *Julius Caesar*, and he did so with *Hamlet* (usually dated about 1600). King Hamlet of Denmark has died, apparently bitten by a poisonous snake. Claudius, his brother, has married the dead king's widow, Gertrude, and become the new king, to the disgust and horror of Prince Hamlet. The ghost of old Hamlet appears to young Hamlet, reveals that he was actually poisoned by Claudius, and demands revenge. Hamlet accepts this as his duty, but cannot bring himself to kill his hated uncle. What follows is Shakespeare's most brilliant and controversial plot.

The story of *Hamlet* is set against the religious controversies of the Bard's time. Is the ghost in hell or purgatory? Is Hamlet Catholic or Protestant? Can revenge ever be justified? We are never really given the answers to such questions. But the play reverberates with them.

THE KING'S MEN

In 1603 Queen Elizabeth I died, and King James VI of Scotland became King James I of England. He also became the patron of Shakespeare's acting company, so the Lord Chamberlain's Men became the King's Men. From this point on, we know less of Shakespeare's life in London than in Stratford, where he kept acquiring property.

In the later years of the sixteenth century Shakespeare had been a rather elusive figure in London, delinquent in paying taxes. From 1602 to 1604 he lived, according to his own later testimony, with a French immigrant family named Mountjoy. After 1604 there is no record of any London residence for Shakespeare, nor do we have any reliable recollection of him or his whereabouts by others. As always, the documents leave much to be desired.

Nearly as great as *Hamlet* is *Othello*, and many regard *King Lear*, the heart-breaking tragedy about an old king and his three daughters, as Shakespeare's supreme tragedy. Shakespeare's shortest tragedy, *Macbeth*, tells the story of a Scottish lord and his wife who plot to murder the king of Scotland to gain the throne for themselves. *Antony and Cleopatra*, a sequel to *Julius Caesar*, depicts the aging Mark Antony in love with the enchanting queen of Egypt. *Coriolanus*, another Roman tragedy, is the poet's least popular masterpiece.

SONNETS AND THE END

The year 1609 saw the publication of Shakespeare's Sonnets. Of these 154 puzzling love poems, the first 126 are addressed to a handsome young man, unnamed, but widely believed to be the Earl of Southampton; the rest concern a dark woman, also unidentified. These mysteries are still debated by scholars.

Near the end of his career Shakespeare turned to comedy again, but it was a comedy of a new and more serious kind. Magic plays a large role in these late plays. For example, in *The Tempest*, the exiled duke of Milan, Prospero, uses magic to defeat his enemies and bring about a final reconciliation.

According to the most commonly accepted view, Shakespeare, not yet fifty, retired to Stratford around 1610. He died prosperous in 1616, and left a will that divided his goods, with a famous provision leaving his wife "my second-best bed." He was buried in the chancel of the parish church, under a tombstone bearing a crude rhyme:

> GOOD FRIEND, FOR JESUS SAKE FORBEARE
> TO DIG THE DUST ENCLOSED HERE.
> BLEST BE THE MAN THAT SPARES THESE STONES,
> AND CURSED BE HE THAT MOVES MY BONES.

This epitaph is another hotly debated mystery: Did the great poet actually compose these lines himself?

SHAKESPEARE'S GRAVE IN HOLY TRINITY CHURCH, STRATFORD-UPON-AVON. HIS WIFE, ANNE HATHAWAY, IS BURIED BESIDE HIM.

THE FOLIO

In 1623 Shakespeare's colleagues of the King's Men produced a large volume of the plays (excluding the sonnets and other poems) titled *The Comedies, Histories, and Tragedies of Mr. William Shakespeare* with a woodcut portrait—the only known portrait—of the Bard. As a literary monument it is priceless, containing our only texts of half the plays; as a source of biographical information it is severely disappointing, giving not even the dates of Shakespeare's birth and death.

Ben Jonson, then England's poet laureate, supplied a long prefatory poem saluting Shakespeare as the equal of the great classical Greek tragedians Aeschylus, Sophocles, and Euripides, adding that "He was not of an age, but for all time."

Some would later denigrate Shakespeare. His reputation took more than a century to conquer Europe, where many regarded him as semi-barbarous. His works were not translated before 1740. Jonson himself, despite his personal affection, would deprecate "idolatry" of the Bard. For a time Jonson himself was considered more "correct" than Shakespeare, and possibly the superior artist.

But Jonson's generous verdict is now the whole world's. Shakespeare was not merely of his own age, "but for all time."

SPEAK ME FAIR IN DEATH.

A GLOSSARY OF LITERARY TERMS

allegory—a story in which characters and events stand for general moral truths. Shakespeare never uses this form simply, but his plays are full of allegorical elements.

alliteration—repetition of one or more initial sounds, especially consonants, as in the saying "through thick and thin," or in Julius Caesar's statement, "veni, vidi, vici."

allusion—a reference, especially when the subject referred to is not actually named, but is unmistakably hinted at.

aside—a short speech in which a character speaks to the audience, unheard by other characters on the stage.

comedy—a story written to amuse, using devices such as witty dialogue (high comedy) or silly physical movement (low comedy). Most of Shakespeare's comedies were romantic comedies, incorporating lovers who endure separations, misunderstandings, and other obstacles but who are finally united in a happy resolution.

deus ex machina—an unexpected, artificial resolution to a play's convoluted plot. Literally, "god out of a machine."

dialogue—speech that takes place among two or more characters.

diction—choice of words for tone. A speech's diction may be dignified (as when a king formally addresses his court), comic (as when the ignorant grave diggers debate whether Ophelia deserves a religious funeral), vulgar, romantic, or whatever the dramatic occasion requires. Shakespeare was a master of diction.

Elizabethan—having to do with the reign of Queen Elizabeth I, from 1558 until her death in 1603. This is considered the most famous period in the history of England, chiefly because of Shakespeare and other noted authors (among them Sir Philip Sidney, Edmund Spenser, and Christopher Marlowe). It was also an era of military glory, especially the defeat of the huge Spanish Armada in 1588.

Globe—the Globe Theater housed Shakespeare's acting company, the Lord Chamberlain's Men (later known as the King's Men). Built in 1598, it caught fire and burned down during a performance of *Henry VIII* in 1613.

hyperbole—an excessively elaborate exaggeration used to create special emphasis or a comic effect, as in Montague's remark that his son Romeo's sighs are "adding to clouds more clouds" in *Romeo and Juliet*.

irony—a discrepancy between what a character says and what he or she truly believes, what is expected to happen and what really happens, or between what a character says and what others understand.

metaphor—a figure of speech in which one thing is identified with another, such as when Hamlet calls his father a "fair mountain." (See also **simile**.)

monologue—a speech delivered by a single character.

motif—a recurrent theme or image, such as disease in *Hamlet* or moonlight in *A Midsummer Night's Dream*.

oxymoron—a phrase that combines two contradictory terms, as in the phrase "sounds of silence" or Hamlet's remark, "I must be cruel only to be kind."

personification—imparting personality to something impersonal ("the sky wept"); giving human qualities to an idea or an inanimate object, as in the saying "love is blind."

pun—a playful treatment of words that sound alike, or are exactly the same, but have different meanings. In *Romeo and Juliet* Mercutio says, after being fatally wounded, "Ask for me tomorrow and you shall find me a grave man." "Grave" could mean either a place of burial or serious.

simile—a figure of speech in which one thing is compared to another, usually using the word *like* or *as*. (See also **metaphor**.)

soliloquy—a speech delivered by a single character, addressed to the audience. The most famous are those of Hamlet, but Shakespeare uses this device frequently to tell us his characters' inner thoughts.

symbol—a visible thing that stands for an invisible quality, as poison in *Hamlet* stands for evil and treachery.

syntax—sentence structure or grammar. Shakespeare displays amazing variety of syntax, from the sweet simplicity of his songs to the clotted fury of his great tragic heroes, who can be very difficult to understand at a first hearing. These effects are deliberate; if we are confused, it is because Shakespeare means to confuse us.

theme—the abstract subject or message of a work of art, such as revenge in *Hamlet* or overweening ambition in *Macbeth*.

tone—the style or approach of a work of art. The tone of *A Midsummer Night's Dream*, set by the lovers, Bottom's crew, and the fairies, is light and sweet. The tone of *Macbeth*, set by the witches, is dark and sinister.

tragedy—a story that traces a character's fall from power, sanity, or privilege. Shakespeare's well-known tragedies include *Hamlet, Macbeth,* and *Othello*.

tragicomedy—a story that combines elements of both tragedy and comedy, moving a heavy plot through twists and turns to a happy ending.

verisimilitude—having the appearance of being real or true.

understatement—a statement expressing less than intended, often with an ironic or comic intention; the opposite of hyperbole.

SHAKESPEARE AND
THE MERCHANT OF VENICE

A nineteenth-century playbill ▶
advertises a benefit featuring
actor Edmund Kean's talents in a
variety of roles, including Shylock
in *The Merchant of Venice*.

PLAY-HOUSE

Mr. KEA[N]

FAREWELL BENEFI[T]
Previous to his departure for America.

MONDAY NEXT, JULY 19th, 1830,

When will be presented FIVE SEPARATE ACTS of those Plays in which Mr. KEAN has been most celebrated.
Commencing with the FOURTH ACT of

Richard the Third,
Richard the Third, Mr. KEAN.
The FOURTH ACT of The
MERCHANT of VENICE.
Shylock, Mr. KEAN.
The FIFTH ACT of
New Way to pay Old Debts.
Sir Giles Overreach, Mr. KEAN.
The SECOND ACT of
MACBETH!
Macbeth, Mr. KEAN.
And the THIRD ACT of
OTHELLO!
Othello, Mr. KEAN.

WITH A VARIETY OF OTHER
ENTERTAINMENTS,
EMBRACING THE
Talent of all his Theatrical Friends now in London.
Particulars of which will be expressed in future Bills.

BOXES, 7s.—PIT, 3s. 6d.—GAL[LERY]

Private Boxes and Tickets may be secured at the Box Office of the Theatre; and at M[r.]
Gloucester Gate, Regent's Park.

66929 **Chapter One** 66929

CHAPTER ONE

Shakespeare and The Merchant of Venice

THE MERCHANT OF VENICE MAKES USE OF SEVERAL DIFFERENT SOURCES, AND, AS IS TYPICAL WITH SHAKESPEARE'S PLAYS, SCHOLARS ARE NOT IN COMPLETE AGREEMENT ON THE PLAYWRIGHT'S REFERENCES. WHAT EVERYONE AGREES ABOUT IS SHAKESPEARE'S ABILITY TO TAKE FOUND STORIES AND MYTHS AND BUILD SOMETHING NEW AND COMPLEX FROM THEM. THE THREE PREEXISTING STORIES IN THE MERCHANT OF VENICE ARE THE RING STORY, THE CASKET STORY, AND THE POUND OF FLESH STORY.

The first has to do with rings given with a promise of fidelity, and then that promise is tested. The casket story is a basic fairy-tale model, with a princess, three caskets, and one lucky prince who chooses the right one, thus earning her hand in marriage. The "pound of flesh" story goes back to antiquity, to either India or Persia. It came to Europe in the twelfth century, and wasn't associated with a Jewish person until the thirteenth century, when it first appeared in England. This was when the Jew as "predator/ creditor" started to take root as a mythical figure. One clear reference for the play is *Il Pecorone* (*The Simpleton*) from fourteenth-century Italy. This story included the pound of flesh component, as well as a lady with her suitors in Belmont, a promise with a ring, and a Jewish moneylender. Christopher Marlowe's drama *The Jew of Malta* from about 1592 represents another of the more obvious connections. There are many plot parallels between these two works, and even some speeches are similar. The "Jew" is perhaps the most striking difference, which helps in the analysis of Shylock in Shakespeare's play, because we can see elaborations and departures on his part that were probably done consciously. Whereas Marlowe depicts a caricature—a simple, greedy villain—Shakespeare offers more depth. Marlowe's moneylender does show cleverness and shrewdness, especially early on, but as the play develops, he ends up as a flat character and one to loathe.

Some consider *The Merchant of Venice* to be one of Shakespeare's first "problem plays," in that it presents controversies of his day in ambiguous ways, leaving the thinking audience perplexed. Elizabethans of Shakespeare's time struggled with the balance between justice and mercy in what was a very litigious age, and also with money-lending or "usury," which was common. Shakespeare's company relied on loans, as did his personal family wealth. There was a discomfort with this, however, and a common belief that too much of it, charging too high an interest, made the practice evil. The play also carries an unclear quality somewhere in between comedy and tragedy. Norrie Epstein lists three plays—*All's Well that Ends Well*, *Troilus and Cressida*, and *Measure for Measure*—as the titles for this type of play. Note her definition of the problem play, however, and how closely Merchant fits:

> . . . THEY ARE PUNGENT SATIRES ON HUMAN VICE, SEXUALITY, FOLLY, AND GREED. TODAY WE WOULD CALL THEM "BLACK COMEDIES," BECAUSE THEY MAKE US LAUGH AT WHAT WE WOULD NORMALLY FIND DISTASTEFUL. NEITHER PURELY COMIC NOR PURELY TRAGIC, THEY FALL INTO A DISTURBINGLY AMBIVALENT LIMBO WHICH IS WHY THEY ARE CONSIDERED PROBLEMATICAL. . . .

It is difficult to determine whether the play is a comedy or a tragedy. The term comedy implies a neat, tidy plot with a light and happy ending, but does not mean that serious themes do not run throughout. A tragedy, on the other hand, may have a messy, unhappy ending and serious commentary on human nature, but this does not preclude the existence of levity. Tragedies tend to follow a trajectory toward death. Comedies may begin with feuding, unhappiness, or confusion, but they end with music and marriage. Young characters often move beyond parental control to a romantic partner. To the Elizabethans, song and dance were symbolic of cosmic harmony, while marriage represented the ideal harmony between the sexes.

According to some critics, Shakespeare interweaves the three borrowed subplots awkwardly: the casket, the bond, and the ring stories. This, too, makes the play "problematic." On the other hand, an argument could be made for the "appearance versus reality" theme, one found in almost every Shakespeare play, holding the whole work together and creating the depth and complexity that we all love about this playwright. Harold C. Goddard puts it nicely when he says, "Drama . . . must make wide and immediate appeal to a large number of people of ordinary intelligence. . . . What the poet is seeking, on the other hand, is the secret of life . . . ." In *The Merchant of Venice*, we find love, suspense, mixed identities, and a happy ending of sorts, along with many intriguing ambiguities and beautifully astute commentaries on human nature. Is the play purely anti-Semitic? Is Shylock a simplistic "bad guy," or is he a sympathetic character? Is Portia admirable or shallow? Is loyalty absolute or merely relative, and how far should one go to test it?

You will find opinions on both sides of these kinds of debates. Perhaps that is what makes Shakespeare so much fun. Today, the challenge is not so much in finding interesting ways of looking at Shakespeare's plays. There is too much information out there. The challenge is sifting through it all and forming your own opinion. Be true to his text and true to yourself. That is the way Shakespeare would want it. As you read the play, keep yourself open and form your own views.

In terms of anti-Semitism, the play can be difficult for a modern reader to accept, and because of this, *The Merchant of Venice* is one of Shakespeare's most controversial plays. Jewish people recount painful memories of having to read it in school. In 1943 a well-known actor, Werner Krauss, was ordered by Joseph Goebbels, Hitler's minister of propaganda, to play Shylock in such a way as to incite hatred against Jews. Since World War II, the play has been banned from many classrooms. In Shakespeare's day, there was also a strong anti-Jewish sentiment. Venice required Jews to live in a walled area with a gate that locked and was guarded by Christians (the first "ghetto"). If a Jew went out past curfew, he was required to wear a red hat to identify him. Jews were not allowed to own property. Their main source of revenue, usury or money-lending, was technically illegal and was frowned upon as immoral. In 1594 there was a case involving a Portuguese Jew accused of treason in a complex political plot. Vengeance played a part and the man's innocence was a distinct possibility. Even the queen herself apparently doubted his guilt. During the trial, the fact that the man was Jewish worked against him. He and his cohorts were put to death. Using Jews as scapegoats to purge society of fear or unease is not an uncommon phenomenon, and Shakespeare may have made use of this dramatic situation in order both to appeal to general audiences and also to probe deeper into its origins.

THE PLAY'S THE THING

- OVERVIEW AND ANALYSIS

- LIST OF CHARACTERS

- ANALYSIS OF MAJOR CHARACTERS

A DVD case cover for the ▶
Royal National Theater's
1999 film production,
directed by Trevor Nunn

THE MERCHANT OF VENICE

William Shakespeare

Chapter Two

66929 66929

CHAPTER TWO

The Play's the Thing

ACT I, SCENE 1

OVERVIEW

The opening scene, on a street in Venice, finds Antonio, Salerio, and Solanio talking about Antonio's ships. Unease and suspense are in the air. Antonio is feeling blue, and he doesn't know why. Salerio and Solanio suggest that his ships are worrying him. Wealth based on credit and trade was a scary, uneasy prospect in Shakespeare's time, as it is today. These friends sympathize with the insecurity of counting on luck and weather, not knowing if one day, circumstances will suddenly change and one's fortunes will shift. "Should I go to church / And see the holy edifice of stone / And not bethink me straight of dangerous rocks, / Which touching but my gentle vessel's side / Would scatter all her spices on the stream, / Enrobe the roaring water with my silks, / And in a word, but even now worth this, / And now worth nothing?"

Antonio assures his friends that his fortunes are not all held in one place, and that this is not why he is sad. The friends' next guess is that he is in love, and he brushes this suggestion off as well. We never discover the actual source of his sadness, which gives this character a vague aimlessness.

Bassanio, Lorenzo, and Gratiano join the group and the mood lifts some. Gratiano notices that Antonio seems out of sorts. He tries to cheer up his friend while playfully goading him. Gratiano talks of supposedly wise men who say very little, but once they do speak, it is revealed that they aren't so wise after all. Lorenzo teases Gratiano for talking so much that he can't get a word in edgewise. The others leave Antonio and Bassanio alone. First, the two jest about Gratiano's vapid conversation. This character offers a light touch and source of humor, but Shakespeare's "fools" often possess wisdom. Here Antonio's sadness is set aside as soon as he hears about his friend's love affair and his need for a loan.

Bassanio has overspent, and now he needs a decent sum of money in order to woo Portia. He talks of her many virtues (including her wealth), and the sense that he and she have a connection. Without hesitation, Antonio is happy to oblige his dear friend's needs. Because his money is tied up, he will need to use his credit to secure a loan for Bassanio. Here the feeling of unease, of credit stretching too thin, increases, but so does the power and generosity of Antonio's friendship. Now that Portia has been introduced in conversation, it is time to meet her.

ANALYSIS

Antonio's fortunes are unsure or suspended, as they hang in part on his ships completing their journey safely, although he assures his friends that his fortune is well distributed and well protected, and Bassanio, who already owes Antonio money, wants to borrow more. This both sets the scene for the central moneylending plot, and also brings up the money theme, how much it determines a person's life, happiness, and relationships with others. Money language is used throughout the play.

This scene explores friendship and its value. Salerio comments, "I would have stay'd till I had made you merry, / If worthier friends had not prevented me", and Antonio reassures him, "Your worth is very dear in my regard." Interestingly, *worth* is a word that could be used to discuss money, so here we see the question of how people value one another, and how much wealth powers friendships. The friendship between Antonio and Bassanio is arguably the strongest, most steady relationship in the entire play. Notice how Antonio perks up and drops talk of sadness upon Bassanio's arrival and the chance for Antonio to help his friend. Says Antonio: "My purse, my person my extremest means / Lie all unlock'd to your occasions." Again friendship accompanies financial offerings. A bit later, when Bassanio worries about the risks Antonio takes in order to offer him the loan he needs, Antonio replies, "To wind about my love with circumstance / And out of doubt you do me now more wrong / In making question of my uttermost / Than if you had made waste of all I have." In other words, his friendship and devoted loyalty are both measured by money and also surpass financial considerations. When Bassanio describes Portia, the word *worth* is also used.

The theme of appearance versus reality is introduced when Antonio comments that the world is "A stage, where every man must play a part, / And mine a sad one." This continues with Gratiano, who plays with words but says nothing—"Gratiano speaks an infinite deal of nothing"—yet he also challenges silence and words, and how those who speak little and are taken as wise might not be. Perhaps, too, in Bassanio's description of

Portia, there is a question about her inner and outer worth and beauty. In one breath, Bassanio describes her beauty, her virtues, and her wealth. Is his judgment of Portia sound and fair? Does language adequately reflect reality? Bassanio mentions "fair speechless messages" that he supposedly received from her. Is this wishful thinking, or can he rely on a sense of her interest that goes beyond or without words?

ACT I, SCENE 2

OVERVIEW

At her house in Belmont, Portia, parallel to Antonio, is feeling inexplicably weary of life. Nerissa, her maid, comments that Portia would truly be unhappy

MICHELLE DUNCAN (PORTIA) AND KIRSTY BESTERMAN (NERISSA) PERFORM AT SHAKESPEARE'S GLOBE THEATER, 2007.

if "your miseries were in the same abundance as your good fortunes are: and yet for aught I see, they are as sick that surfeit with too much, as they that starve with nothing." Here is a lesson as apt today as it was in Shakespeare's day: that those who have too much keep wanting more, and there is a sickness in society from such excess. An often-quoted speech follows, when Portia says, "If to do were as easy as to know what were good to do, chapels had been churches, and poor men's cottages princes' palaces." If only we all could actually do what we know is right! While following the rules, the casket competition has grown tedious for Portia.

Nerissa seems to have more faith in the father's wisdom and the happy results of the test. A humorous litany follows, however, of all of the losers who have come to take the test, and luckily for Portia, all will be leaving her soon.

Interestingly, it is Nerissa who first brings up Bassanio, and describes him as the best choice. Portia agrees. We leave Portia to greet another suitor, and then are introduced to Shylock.

ANALYSIS

Can money buy happiness? The two most prominent characters in terms of wealth are the two least happy: Antonio and Portia, and it is only in giving money away that they gain some contentment. This also overlaps with the theme of appearance versus reality, as one may appear to have everything one wants, and yet still not feel satisfied.

While Portia acknowledges the wisdom of Nerrisa's words about having no reason for sadness, can she act on them? She mentions that it is easier to offer wisdom than follow it; this becomes a stronger issue much later in the play, particularly in the trial scene.

That Portia and Nerissa both favor Bassanio could mean that they can both see past appearances to the qualities that Portia wants and deserves, or that they are both somehow won over by Bassanio's outward charm and looks. Perhaps, as Nerissa suggests, it is simply destiny.

There are two strained father-daughter relationships in this play: that of Portia and her deceased father, and that of Shylock and Jessica. In Portia's case, her husband will not be chosen by her, but through a test devised by her father. Here is where the "casket story" enters. This is the most obvious manifestation of the appearance versus reality theme, as her suitors must choose from a gold, silver, and lead casket. The correct guess will bring the reward of Portia's hand in marriage. Portia is resentful of the restriction and is tired of the game. Portia is the more loyal of the two daughters, yet both are rewarded by the end. Is it more acceptable in this world to be rebellious when one is fighting against a Jewish father and his culture?

ACT I, SCENE 3

OVERVIEW

This scene at a public place in Venice starts right in the middle of the action, with Bassanio arranging with Shylock to borrow his wooing money, using Antonio's fortune as collateral. Some say that Shakespeare writes in a way that reminds one of the way films are done, which is pretty incredible, given that he predates the camera, let alone moving pictures. His work is timeless in so many ways! Antonio shows up, and Shylock offers all his hatred in an aside, where he lists the merchant's offenses. First, he is Christian. In addition, he lends money for free and brings down Shylock's rates. Third, he hates all Jews ("our sacred nation") and he criticizes Shylock's business practices in public. Some bickering follows, in which Shylock proudly cites the Bible and his ancestry, and

I LIKE NOT FAIR TERMS AND A VILLAIN'S MIND.

Antonio shows his impatience. Antonio is starting to feel uneasy and suspicious. The negotiations continue, but when pushed, Shylock cannot resist complaining about the terrible treatment he has had to suffer in the past. Perhaps this is an opening for some kind of sympathy from Antonio, or perhaps this is one more step in the inevitable, entrenched hatred between these two characters. Antonio offers none of the former and plenty of the latter, suggesting that there is no possibility of friendship, so if Shylock is going to lend the money, it may as well be to an enemy and not a friend.

Then comes the brutal bond: Shylock suggests a forfeit of a pound of Antonio's flesh if he does not meet the deadline for repayment. Bassanio is afraid, but Antonio is confident.

ANALYSIS

Although he is not a simple character, Shylock is not easy to like. In this scene, he repeats the amount of the loan, "three thousand ducats," revealing his obsession with money. When he concedes that Antonio is a "good" man, Shylock equates this with his worth instead of his character, offering the word *sufficient* instead and then describing his various assets. Again, appearance versus reality comes into play when Shylock dismisses Antonio's wealth as only virtual or provisional: "Yet his means are in supposition . . . . ships are but boards, sailors but men, there be land-rats, and water-rats, water-thieves, and land-thieves." Yet doesn't a Jewish businessman need to be cautious and skeptical, given the way he may be judged and discriminated against? There is also a sense throughout the play that, if only Shylock were more Christian, all would be well. He requests a meeting with Antonio, and is invited to dine with Antonio and Bassanio. Perhaps this is merely a well-meaning, friendly gesture, and Shylock's response is exaggerated and bitter. He says, "Yes, to smell pork, to eat of the habitation which your prophet the Nazarite conjured the devil into: I will buy with you, sell with you, talk with you, walk with you, and so following: but I will not eat with you, drink with you, nor pray with you." But maybe, too, the assumption that Shylock can easily fit himself into Christian culture is presumptuous. Perhaps he is the avaricious Jew, but perhaps, too, it is only in the commercial setting where he can relate to his Christian counterparts. It is not he who created these limitations, but he is keenly aware of them in ways that his Christian peers have the luxury of ignoring.

Shylock's anger is personal, but he also feels that he represents all Jews: "Cursed be my tribe / If I forgive him!" Some argue that Shylock is a nasty, greedy man, a simple bad guy, and that this is separate from his race. Perhaps he uses his Judaism as an excuse for his self-serving hatred of Antonio. Another argument is that this play is anti-Semitic, and that his greed and hatred are made synonymous with his race. This certainly coincides with common thinking of the time. A third view holds that because of the injustices heaped upon Shylock and his people, he is forced into a defensive and suspicious position, and he must fight against Antonio or else lose his livelihood and his racial pride.

A range of interpretations are on offer for Shylock's biblical reference. Shylock may be asserting that human cleverness can always prevail and figure out a way to profit, or he may be hoping for a miracle to aid him in the deal to which he is about to agree. Perhaps he is justifying usury based on his esteemed biblical ancestors. He could be setting the scene for creative lending practices (in the story, it is sheep, whereas here, it will be a pound of human flesh). Antonio proudly reiterates that he lends money out of friendship and does not take interest. While Antonio's tone becomes increasingly frustrated, Shylock dallies calmly in conversation. He even seems to be drawing out the dialogue: "I had forgot—three months." It seems unlikely that he did forget. This is a rare moment when he is in power. Bassanio very much needs his help. The dramatic tension parallels the trial scene, when Portia draws it out to an excruciating degree.

Antonio once again brings up the appearance versus reality theme when he remarks, "The devil can cite scripture for his purpose. An evil soul producing holy witness / Is like a villain with a smiling cheek . . . ." With the talk of friendship, Shylock can play the hurt one, saying that he would have been a friend, if Antonio hadn't "stormed" so. Does he really mean it? Or is he playing up the moment so as better to assert his momentary power?

In Antonio's acceptance of the terms of the loan, we see the power of his friendship with Bassanio and perhaps also his hubris regarding his own luck and fortunes. In both sarcastic bitterness and prophetic wisdom, Antonio comments, "The Hebrew will turn Christian, he grows kind," but Bassanio quips, "I like not fair terms, and a villain's mind." The confusion of suspicion, hatred, and brutality in this exchange foreshadows the trouble to come.

ACT II, SCENE 1

OVERVIEW

In another filmlike move, we switch back to the arrival of the next suitor, with whom we left off when we were last in Belmont with Portia and Nerissa. The prince of Morocco asks not to be judged by his dark complexion. Portia assures him that even if she were free to choose, as she is not, he would stand as fair a chance as any. The prince is grateful and then eager to pick one of the caskets. He uses courageous, perhaps boastful language to describe his physical, warlike prowess, yet he also admits that all of this is for naught, and one less worthy could simply be luckier in winning what he himself loses: Portia.

ANALYSIS

Here we see the theme of appearance versus reality continue, both with the caskets and the dark-skinned prince. There is some irony that he gets better treatment than Shylock, but he is also a minor character, and, since he loses Portia, he is not a threat to her or her way of life the way Shylock is a threat to the surrounding characters. Destiny plays a role again when the prince juxtaposes his merits against the dumb luck of choosing the right casket. While this frustrates him, perhaps Bassanio and Portia's love is already written in the stars, and no luck, wit, or individual achievements can get in the way of that.

ACT II, SCENE 2

OVERVIEW

This scene opens with Launcelot Gobbo, the clown and Shylock's servant, talking to himself on a street in Venice. He wavers back and forth in his decision whether or not to run away, saying how cruel Shylock is, how much like the devil, and yet it is his inner fiend that urges him to run, and his conscience that urges him to stay.

Then Old Gobbo appears, asking directions to Shylock's place. Teasing his near-blind father, Launcelot offers convoluted directions. Old Gobbo asks after Launcelot, and confusion over titles and names ensues, with the son saying he has died, the father sad at the news and not recognizing his son before him. Finally, after some back and forth about Launcelot's beard and how much he has changed, his father acknowledges him. Launcelot is on the run, hoping to switch his services to Bassanio.

OLD GOBBO (LARRINGTON WALKER) AND LAUNCELOT GOBBO (WILLIAM BECK) SHARE A SCENE AT THE COURTYARD THEATER, STRATFORD-UPON-AVON, 2008.

Father and son make a tangled offer to Bassanio, both of the gift that was originally meant for Shylock and of Launcelot's services. Bassanio agrees, mentioning that Shylock is also willing to make this switch.

Gratiano shows up as the father and son team are on their way out. He asks to be included in Bassanio's trip to Belmont. Bassanio says that Gratiano's wild and rude ways are fine in his company, but that he must dress and behave with propriety and civility, so that Portia doesn't get the wrong idea about Bassanio. The friends agree that the evening before them is for fun, and that the seriousness will follow. This hints at the more extreme disguised identities in the trial scene.

ANALYSIS

With Launcelot's opening speech, we find a dizzying confusion and are left wondering what is right, what is wrong, and how is one to know? We are also left with a very unfavorable view of Shylock.

Launcelot worries that "I am a Jew if I serve the Jew any longer." Judaism seems to be contagious here, and the person with whom one allies oneself is of great importance. Notice, too, that all of the familial ties are weaker than those of friendship and romance in this play. Portia is loyal, but she is not free of resentment for her deceased father. Jessica ends up betraying her father. And this comical, estranged pair barely recognizes one another, but the bond between servant and master or friends such as Antonio and Bassanio is most intense indeed. Perhaps the capitalistic system explored by this play, with credit extended to its limit and money as the primary criterion for assessing others is not unlike our current times, and perhaps our current worries about the changing shape of families are not new, either.

In the conversation with Bassanio, Shylock is equated with being godless or devil-like when Launcelot comments that Bassanio has "the grace of god" while Shylock has "enough." Bassanio is in debt, but he is a gentleman and a Christian. Shylock has wealth, but, as a Jewish person, that is not enough to redeem him; in fact, it becomes a source of criticism (and perhaps jealousy).

With Bassanio and Gratiano's dialogue, we see another reference to the theme of appearance versus reality, but here, a person might not simply have one appearance. He may put on clothes and manners to suit the occasion. Do our identities shift as our appearances do? This is carried out further by Portia and Nerissa in the trial scene. That Bassanio is so concerned with Gratiano's appearance demonstrates that people are judged by the company they keep. This is part of Launcelot's concern with working for Shylock.

ACT II, SCENE 3

OVERVIEW

In Shylock's house Jessica says her farewell to Launcelot, sad to see him go, as he added some merriment to a home she says is a hell. They both talk of her "bettering" herself by marrying a Christian. She has sent a note to her beloved, Lorenzo, that the departing servant is meant to deliver in secret. Jessica seems to despise her father, yet acknowledges that a "heinous sin is it in me / To be ashamed to be my father's child!"

ANALYSIS

Jessica gains sympathy from her Christian peers and a Christian audience by criticizing her father and craving escape from his hellish household. It may not be his Judaism, however, that truly troubles her. She is a typical rebellious teen, more bothered perhaps by the "tediousness" (her word) of her home than its cultural or religious identity. She doesn't have many choices if she does want to break away, especially since she is in love with Lorenzo, a Christian gentleman. Still her willingness to convert is part of a movement toward a Christian "happily ever after" conclusion, where Shylock is forced to do so as well.

ACT II, SCENE 4

OVERVIEW

Gratiano, Lorenzo, Salerio, and Solanio discuss preparations for the upcoming party or "masque," which includes elaborate costumes. Launcelot delivers Jessica's letter, and Lorenzo recognizes her handwriting. Lorenzo sends Launcelot back to Jessica with the reply that he will not fail her. While Salerio and Solanio head off to prepare for the festivities, Gratiano and Lorenzo talk about Jessica. Lorenzo shares the plans that Jessica has just set out: She asks that Lorenzo carry her off from her father's home, and she will bring with her all the gold and jewels that she can.

ANALYSIS

Here begins the sequence of disguises and hidden or confused identities, which is part of the appearance versus reality theme. With the loving couples in the play, it seems each is able to see below the surface of the other. Here, the exterior is an envelope, and for Bassanio, it will be the caskets.

Once again, romance goes hand in hand with money. Does Jessica become more appealing because she has wealth to bring with her, or does she feel pressure to do so? Jessica's betrayal of her father is excused by the characters in the play because of his religion. "And never dare misfortune cross her foot, / Unless she do it under this excuse, / That she is issue to a faithless Jew."

ACT II, SCENE 5

OVERVIEW

Launcelot visits Shylock, his old boss, to invite him to dine with Bassanio, his new master. Shylock is grumpy and grudging in his assent, saying that the invitation does not come from friendship: "I am not bid for love, they

GILBERT STUART NEWTON'S 1830 OIL PAINTING, SHYLOCK AND JESSICA FROM THE MERCHANT OF VENICE, IS DISPLAYED AT THE YALE CENTER FOR BRITISH ART.

flatter me. / But yet I'll go in hate." He is especially hesitant because of a dream he had, about moneybags, which causes him worry and Launcelot mirth; he mocks Shylock's superstition.

Shylock asks Jessica to watch the house and keep it locked up, and not even to look out at the foolish Christians and their partying. Launcelot whispers to Jessica about her escape plan and Lorenzo's visit.

After Launcelot's departure, Shylock explains why he is glad to be rid of him. He says that this servant was slow and lazy, "snail-slow in profit" and wishes that he will end up wasting the money of his new master instead, who happens also to be the benefactor of Shylock's loan, Bassanio. Shylock leaves and Jessica is alone with her excitement and anxiety over her plan to run away from home.

ANALYSIS

In his response to the dinner invitation, Shylock shows himself to be either a bitter, unpleasant man who always expects the worst of people, or someone who is used to being treated with mistrust, insincerity, and bigotry, and knows better than to expect friendship. Is he being unfair and paranoid when he asks Jessica to lock all doors and not even to peep out? Certainly not, because when he is not in earshot, Launcelot advises Jessica to do the opposite of her father's bidding, to be on the lookout for a certain Christian gentleman who plans to "rescue" her.

In this scene, the obsession with money resurfaces and the controversy continues. Is Shylock unbearably miserly and greedy, or necessarily thrifty and cautious? The proverb that he quotes, "Fast bind, fast find—A proverb never stale in thrifty mind," could be interpreted either way. He has worked hard to earn, save, and maintain his fortune. It is all he has. And yet maybe he needs to appreciate other things, especially his own daughter, who at that very moment is plotting to leave him. "Farewell—and if my fortune be not crost, I have a father, you a daughter, lost." It is interesting that she talks of money, too, through the pun on the word *fortune* (meaning "luck" or "wealth"). The success of her plan is contingent on her "fortune." And is not Lorenzo greedy, too, accepting her additional burden of coins and jewels as part of the escape plan?

ACT II, SCENE 6

OVERVIEW

The scene continues in front of Shylock's house, where Gratiano and Salerio await Lorenzo, wondering why he is late. If he is pursuing love, shouldn't he be early, not late? Pleasures do not last, and one should not want to waste any time in pursing them. Lorenzo apologizes, claiming, "Not I, but my affairs, have made you wait."

Lorenzo approaches Shylock's house, and Jessica calls down to him. She asks who is there, but recognizes his voice, and they both exchange vows of love. Jessica is glad to be clothed in night, embarrassed by her forward words, and also embarrassed by her disguise in boy's clothes (this foreshadows Portia and Nerissa's later disguise). Lorenzo is not bothered by either, and he welcomes her to join him. Jessica does not come empty-handed; she brings along a significant amount of her father's wealth.

Gratiano approves of Jessica. Lorenzo then outlines his judgment of her, that she has proven herself to be fair, wise, and true. She may be true to him, but she certainly is not true to her father or her heritage.

Antonio appears and announces that there won't be a party after all, and that Bassanio is ready to set sail. Gratiano says he is pleased to get going.

ANALYSIS

Lorenzo's tardiness could hint at some lack of determination on his part, except that all other signs indicate his great love for Jessica and his desire to carry out their escape. These lines could indicate the frivolity of these two characters as foil or contrast with the serious lovers.

Interestingly, as she joins Lorenzo, Jessica says, "I will make fast the doors, and gild myself / With some more ducats," as if she herself is golden, as if she is worthier of her love because of the money she carries.

Gratiano is impressed, calling Jessica "gentle" (also a pun with the word gentile) and "no Jew," so for her to count as a viable mate for his friend, as a respectable woman, she cannot also be Jewish. Most of the obviously anti-Semitic comments come from minor characters, with the exception of Antonio. This could be Shakespeare's way of dismissing or critiquing such sentiments, juxtaposing them against more subtle and tolerant views.

Earlier, Gratiano was happy about the party or masque. Now he is happy not to go, because Bassanio is on his way to Belmont (where, it will turn out, Nerissa is waiting for Gratiano).

ACT II, SCENE 7

We switch back again to Portia and the prince of Morocco, which draws out the suspense of his task. Now the time has come for him to choose a casket. He passes up the lead one, as the inscription announces "Who chooseth me must give and hazard all he hath." Why take risks merely for lead? The prince esteems himself quite highly, better than lead: "A golden mind stoops not to shows of dross, / I'll then nor give nor hazard aught for lead." The silver casket tempts him. "Who chooseth me, shall get as much as he deserves." He convinces himself that in fortune, breeding and love, he surely does deserve this lady. He takes a look at the gold one, and finds, "Who chooseth me shall gain what many men desire," and is sure that men the world over desire Portia. He then makes the mistake of equating the woman with outward appearances, the materials of the boxes, and decides that lead and silver are not worthy of her.

Morocco opens the casket to find a skull and a scroll. The often-quoted proverb begins the note: "All that glisters (glitters) is not gold." The note continues to berate him for being more bold than wise. With deep sadness and disappointment, the prince rushes off.

ANALYSIS

This scene builds up the suspense and moves the fairy tale forward. Three suitors will try the test and the magic number three will mark the victor. We also see the theme of appearance versus reality shine forth. For Morocco, the outward appearances of the caskets carry too much meaning. He seems also to judge himself and perhaps Portia, too, by outward trappings of wealth and breeding. He is thinking about what he can get, not what he can give, and for all of these reasons, is a loser. After his departure, Portia comments again about his "complexion." Is she snidely canceling her earlier assurance of not being bothered by his dark skin? There is a hint of this, a hint that her words do not always reflect her true feelings. This is another version of that same theme, the surface of words, opposed to the hidden meanings below them. Shakespeare toys with this throughout the play.

ACT II, SCENE 8

OVERVIEW

Back in Venice, we are thrust into the middle of the action again, with Salerio and Solanio discussing Jessica's escape. Bassanio's ship was under suspicion, but Antonio vouched for him that Jessica was not on board. The duke was informed that the two lovers were spotted in a gondola. Shylock's response is reported and critiqued. He yells "My daughter! O my ducats! O my daughter! / Fled with a Christian! O my Christian ducats!"

Salerio prophetically remarks, "Let good Antonio look he keep his day, / Or he shall pay for this," demonstrating that Shylock's rage and later vengeful resolve do indeed stem from the hurt and anger over this betrayal. They discuss some bad shipping news, and worry about Antonio's fortunes. Salerio then reports what a kind and loyal friend Antonio is, that he generously suggested that Bassanio spend as long as he wants with the woman he loves and not even think about his friend's bond, and that they shook hands as Antonio fought back tears. These two men admire Antonio and look out for him, wishing him the best and hoping to keep him in good cheer.

ANALYSIS

On one level, the daughter and ducat quote indicates that Shylock is obsessed with money (but do keep in mind that this is second-hand, not spoken directly by him), as worried about his money as his daughter. But on another level, the fact that his daughter has run off with a Christian is a blow to his entire faith, and the depletion of his funds—the only source of respect and power that he has—marks a loss that is more than just monetary.

Antonio is presented as a contrast to Shylock—he is loyal to a fault, confident of his fortunes, while Shylock is alone, recently bereft of daughter and jewels, ungenerous and cautious with his wealth. Antonio is a warm, amenable fellow who inspires such friendship and loyalty, but Shylock is isolated and does not seem to have the chance for such support. Perhaps Antonio should pay more attention to his business and less to Shylock. Antonio seems only to care about Bassanio: "I think he only loves the world for him." In a way, Bassanio represents Antonio's sole purpose for living, and if so, there is something dangerous or wrong with this (not in terms of the homosexual overtones, but in terms of his lacking other interests and values). Antonio might hold on to his fortune better if he cared more, and Shylock might hold on to his daughter if he cared more. That these two characters are opposites and enemies, and that both make mistakes of extremity, serves as a call for balance. In most aspects of life—eating, playing, working, loving—we are often reminded to seek balance and moderation.

ACT II, SCENE 9

OVERVIEW

At Belmont we are already on to the next prince, Arragon, and Portia is called quickly to witness his performance. Portia and Arragon review the rules of the "competition." Quickly he dismisses the lead box and, soon after, the gold one. He says that "many men" would include too wide a group, fools who judge only by their eyes. He does not want to be ranked among the common masses. The silver box is his choice. He seems sure that many do not earn their titles or truly deserve Portia, but he does. Unfortunately for him, this turns out not to be the case. He finds there a

JOHN WILLIAM GODWARD'S *NERISSA* IS AN EXAMPLE OF THE NEOCLASSICAL 'MARBLE SCHOOL' PAINTING STYLE OF THE LATE NINETEENTH AND EARLY TWENTIETH CENTURY.

picture of a fool. Shocked, he asks if this is really what he deserves. Portia replies with another proverb, "To offend and judge are distinct offices, / And of opposed natures." Judgment should be neutral, wise, and free of bias, anger, or frustration. To give or take offense is not to be free of the bias and anger needed for wisdom. Arragon, Morocco, and others like them are short on wisdom and, therefore, their judgments are suspect. Ironically Shakespeare challenges the judgment of the major characters, too, including Portia. Arragon rushes off in embarrassment.

Portia is tired and irritated with her suitors thus far, saying that it is their own fault, their lack of wisdom, that ends up leading to frustration. Nerissa replies that destiny is what really determines the outcome, and then, as timing would have it, the next suitor's arrival is announced (Bassanio). It soon will be his turn to test his destiny. The messenger describes the suitor with great enthusiasm. Portia cuts him off, wishing to view this new suitor. Nerissa follows, secretly hoping it is Bassanio.

ANALYSIS

Arragon perhaps does a bit better than Morrocco, showing understanding of the "all that glitters is not gold" proverb without having to encounter it, and yet, it is his pride in himself, not his appreciation of Portia, that moves him to reject the golden casket. He touches again on the contrast between appearances and reality when he says, "for who shall go about / To cozen Fortune, and be honorable / Without the stamp of merit?—let none presume / To wear an undeserved dignity." He knows that some show outward signs of nobility or merit that are not necessarily true, and yet he still feels that this does not apply to him. When Portia contrasts the term *offend* with the term *judge*, she offers a hint of judicial concerns that will appear in the fourth act. Judgment should be fair, clean of cruelty or offense, pure in some way. Her assertion takes on an ironic twist with her behavior in the courtroom.

While the suitors who seem fixated on appearance lose the contest, Bassanio is appreciated partly because of his rich appearance. The messenger equates his wealth with his worthiness when he says, ". . . Gifts of rich value; / yet I have not seen so likely an ambassador of love." In her impatience Portia reveals a similar bias: "I long to see / Quick Cupid's post that comes so mannerly." Nerissa is excited, too, and hopes the suitor is Bassanio. Just as Gratanio approved of Jessica, here Nerissa welcomes Bassanio as Portia's possible spouse. The judgment of friends is a nice, perhaps needed, affirmation. But Nerissa reminds Portia, and all of us, too, that no matter how we judge or scheme, love is a matter of destiny: "The ancient saying is no heresy: / Hanging and wiving goes by destiny."

ACT III, SCENE 1

OVERVIEW

In Venice, Salerio and Solanio talk about the loss of one of Antonio's ships, just as they had foretold in the very first scene. There is also some levity with puns and jokes about gossipy or untrustworthy women and a play on the word *end*, with Salerio asking his friend to get to the end of his point, and the other replying that he hopes this marks the end of Antonio's losses. They note the arrival of Shylock with unpleasant dread, "Let me say amen betimes, lest the devil cross my prayer, for here he comes in the likeness of a Jew."

Shylock angrily confronts these two with the fact that they knew about his daughter's escape. Again, while the exchange is about a serious, emotional topic, there is playfulness in the language. Solanio comments that Jessica was full grown (a bird full fledged) and ready to go. There is a play on the words *dam* and *damned*, with Shylock saying she will be damned for this. Then, when he comments on her being his flesh and blood, Solanio teases him by reinterpreting that expression in sexual terms, saying Shylock is too old for that. Salerio comments that Shylock and Jessica are more different than alike (leading again to her acceptance in the Christian world). To add to the animosity and frustration, he taunts Shylock with a question about Antonio's ships.

Shylock shows suspicion at not having seen Antonio lately, and in his already angry state, rants and raves about Antonio and his smugness, and that the bond will be honored. Salerio pushes Shylock even further when he says that there is certainly no use in actually holding Antonio to his agreement and taking a pound of his flesh. Then follows one of the most famous speeches in the play, when Shylock explains his motivation in following through with the once "merry" agreement. Antonio has mocked him, hurt his business, criticized his entire race ("scorned my nation"), turned his friends from him, and all because he is a Jew. He has eyes, hands, organs, all the same parts as Christians. If a Christian is wronged, he'll seek vengeance, so why can't a Jew do the same?

A messenger then appears to call Solanio and Salerio to Antonio's house. When Tubal, Shylock's friend, arrives, Solanio makes another reference to the devil: "Here comes another of the tribe—a third cannot be match'd, unless the devil himself turn Jew."

Shylock asks Tubal about Jessica, and receives only bad news. She cannot be found. Shylock expresses great anger and frustration, perhaps masking hurt, saying he would rather she were dead at his feet than escaped with his jewels. He bemoans the loss of money both with her escape and with the efforts to find her. The good news is that one of Antonio's ships was lost. Shylock actually thanks God for this, which does not make him look very good. Tubal then offers more painful news about Jessica, that she is spending wildly, and actually traded the ring of beloved Leah, Shylock's deceased wife, for a monkey. Tubal ends by cheering

Shylock up with a reminder that Antonio too has suffered a loss, and will likely not be able to return the loan. Shylock is glad of this, and spurred to action, setting a plan in motion and commenting that with Antonio out of the way, his business will thrive.

ANALYSIS

Throughout the play, Shylock is associated with the devil, and here we see that in very unsubtle terms. The separation of Jessica from Shylock pushes plot and thematic elements. It allows her to move closer to the Christian world, as highlighted here by Salerio's comment that father and daughter do not seem to be of the same blood. It also provides the primary motivation for Shylock to take the bond literally and seek vengeance against Antonio. The merchant had already represented more than a commercial rival for Shylock. As someone who spat upon and looked down on Shylock, he represents all Christians who won't accept Shylock or any Jewish person. At the same time, this becomes not just general, but very personal, because of the loss of Shylock's daughter. Solanio and Salerio's taunts, as well as Tubal's news about the lost ship, are all that Shylock needs to combine all of his rage and pain in the pursuit of his bond. Oddly he uses the word *vengeance* when he talks of Jessica. His speech here is a disturbing one, as he spends more time talking about the financial loss associated with her departure and the efforts to find her than the loss of his daughter. He also wishes her dead at his feet instead of lost with his jewels. Yet he also talks of burying her with the jewels. Shylock seems to think only of money, and at the same time, he looks not just at its face value, but at what it represents: power, security, and loyalty. Jessica betrayed him in two ways: first by running away with a Christian, thus denying her father and her heritage; and second by absconding with much of his wealth. Perhaps the fact that Shylock talks of burying the jewels indicates his inner conflict between his fatherly instincts and his miserly ones, and he wishes his miserly self to be buried and gone.

Vengeance, wealth, power, and heartbreak are interwoven in a painful, dizzying frenzy in the exchange with Tubal, as he talks of Antonio, then Jessica, and back and forth, feeding Shylock bits of information at a time, leading up to the most painful betrayal, that Jessica sold Shylock's dead wife's ring for a trivial monkey. Finally Tubal concludes with the comment that Antonio "is certainly undone," thus leaving Shylock with the clear mission of vengeance.

Shylock offers the powerful speech in this scene that is a primary source of sympathy for him, and yet he still does not come across so well. He seems unable to address the deep and personal pain of the loss of his daughter, and instead focuses on financial issues. He mentions God only when thankful of Antonio's predicament, and plans to meet at the synagogue not to worship, but to make plans for Antonio's destruction. Even that plan is not discussed in terms of retribution for terrible, racist wrongs, but in mercantile terms. It would be good for business. It could be spirituality in general that is at stake here, however, not merely Shylock's faith. In the "Hath not a Jew eyes?" speech, Shylock mentions that Christians and Jews alike seek vengeance. Similar to the synagogue reference here, in the very first scene, Salerio refers to a church, but only in terms of how an architectural element reminds him of a rock at sea and possible damage to ships. It is the whole commercial world of Venice that seems to represent a challenge to virtuous living, not just the Jewish moneylender.

ACT III, SCENE 2

OVERVIEW

At Belmont again Portia and Bassanio are together, and yet they are not. He has to pass the test first. She gives a long speech about wanting to stall the process, because she might lose him, while before he takes the test, at least he is with her. She apologizes for talking so much, yet does so. She bemoans the fact that she has to follow rules and cannot be completely his. She is tempted to break the rules, but does not. Bassanio cannot wait, however. The suspense is agonizing for him. Portia then expresses suspicion and misgivings. "Upon the rack Bassanio? Then confess / What treason there is mingled with your love." He assures her that his love is true and pure, and she is appeased. Portia then requests music as background to his endeavor. Depending on the outcome, the music can play a different role. It can add to the mood of sadness and defeat if he loses, her tears mingling with the tune, or if he wins, it will be wedding music. She refers to Hercules, who rescued a Trojan princess not for love, but for the horses promised to him by the king of Troy. She implies that Bassanio is more true a lover than this.

The little tune that she sings along to happens to have end rhymes that rhyme with "lead." She could be offering a sneaky clue for Bassanio here, or else the hint is for the audience.

Bassanio then speaks of outward courage, outward beauty which mask the opposite. He is not moved by the "gaudy gold," but instead goes for the lead casket, which does not offer gifts, but asks that the one selecting it be the giver.

In an aside, Portia is ecstatic, overwhelmed by her own emotions. All petty feelings that tarnish love, such as jealousy, fear, or despair vanish.

Bassanio opens the casket to find a picture of Portia. He is the winner! First he praises the picture, and wonders how the artist could have done such a good job, especially with her eyes. Wouldn't viewing one entrance

TELL ME WHERE IS FANCY BRED, IN THE HEART OR IN THE HEAD?

HOW BEGOT, HOW NOURISHED? REPLY, REPLY.

him so that he couldn't finish the other one? But then Bassanio notes that the real Portia puts the picture to shame. The scroll inside congratulates him for seeing past surface appearances, asks him to accept his prize and look no further, and grants him permission to kiss his bride. Bassanio cannot believe his good luck, and needs the kiss to confirm that it is true.

Portia says she is not worthy of him, and wishes she was much more, but is willing to learn from him and do her best to please him. She says that all that is hers is now his, and offers him her ring, saying that parting from it means parting from her and life. Bassanio takes the ring and accepts the promise.

Gratiano then asks permission also to be wed. He has already found Nerissa. They apparently have made a deal that if Bassanio was to win Portia, Nerissa would give herself to Gratiano. Portia asks her maid if this is indeed true, and Nerissa confirms the agreement. Nerissa and Gratiano have Portia and Basssanio's blessings. Then, Lorenzo, Jessica, and Salerio appear.

Bassanio receives a letter from Antonio with very bad news. Portia notices her lover's pale face and knows this before hearing it. Antonio's ships have all faltered, and Shylock is not interested in the money anyway. He is insisting that the bond be honored. Bassanio admits to Portia with shame that he not only "was nothing" as he had said when wooing her, but less than that, because he was in debt to Antonio. Portia immediately asks how much is owed, offers to pay twenty times that, and says that, after their marriage, Bassanio should take her money and go fix this problem, while she and Nerissa will wait virtuously (living as "maids and widows").

Portia asks to hear the letter. Bassanio reads aloud that Antonio expects to die, and only requests one last chance to see Bassanio, but only if Bassanio himself truly wants to, only if he truly loves Antonio. Portia urges Bassanio to get going and take care of this, and he is off, promising his loyalty to her as he goes.

ANALYSIS

Portia plays the coy, submissive lady here, yet contradicts such an image at the same time. She apologizes for talking too much, but does so anyway. She claims a passive obedience to her father's dictated casket trick, yet offers a clue to Bassanio through the background song. She describes herself as unworthy of Bassanio, yet is quick to use her wealth to fix Antonio's problem. Oddly she says, "Since you are dear bought, I will love you dear." This could simply mean that it was so difficult to finally get Bassanio as her husband, that she treasures him even more. *Dear* is another money term, though, as is *bought*, of course. Portia seems unabashed about her wealth and what it means and brings her. She got the man she wants, and now she will use her wealth to keep him happy. She offers to wait quietly for his return, but clearly her complicated plan is already starting to form. Portia passionately loves Bassanio, but is a quick thinker and practical problem-solver as well.

Portia is not only smart and powerful, but generous, too. Antonio stands between her and Bassanio in a way, yet she immediately offers to do whatever it takes to help him, and honors his longing, loving request to see Bassanio again.

Bassanio is rewarded for being one character who does not judge a book by its cover. He chooses the most humble casket, the lead one. Yet he is also wooing Portia, who is both beautiful and wealthy.

There is disagreement among scholars about Lorenzo and Jessica's arrival, since she is not given a greeting. Some note a disruption of the lines' rhythm, which could indicate editing and lost versions, or else lines have been dropped to keep the action moving quickly. A third interpretation is that Jessica, still a Jewish person and therefore an outsider, is ignored by all, especially Portia. Gratiano does refer to her as an "infidel."

Music is important to Shakespeare. It appears again in the last act. Here, it not only sets a mood, but actually predicts or determines a plot element. Music moves people and the story, and it represents harmony in the universe. The only suitor who is given music is the one whom Portia wants, and the one who wins her.

ACT III, SCENE 3

OVERVIEW

Antonio with the jailer (Gaoler) encounters a very angry Shylock on a street in Venice. Antonio tries to start up a conversation with Shylock, but he will not have it. He simply repeats the refrain that he will have his bond. Antonio then backs off, saying it is useless to try to reason with Shylock. Solanio tries to reassure him, saying the duke would never let the terrible bond go through, but Antonio replies that the law must be honored. Venice relies on the international world of business, and therefore, must adhere to laws and apply those to all concerned, or else these commercial connections will be destroyed.

ANALYSIS

In one interpretation, Shylock is sinking toward madness, and thus we see his usual speech pattern of rhythmic prose with repetition go further, into almost senseless repetition: "I'll have my bond." Perhaps he can't even hear Antonio at this point. Another view would hold that his built-up anger from being mistreated by everyone has now found its focus and release, so he

IF YOU PRICK US, DO WE NOT BLEED?

is bent on vengeance against Antonio, the spokesperson or representative of those injustices. Antonio also, of course, ruins Shylock's business, as he himself points out here: "I oft deliver'd from his forfeitures / Many that have at times made moan to me, / Therefore he hates me." Yet is it Antonio who is oversimplifying? Shylock earlier says, "Thou call'dst me dog before thou hadst a cause, / But since I am a dog, beware my fangs," touching on the self-fulfilling prophecy often found in racist environments. If a group is assumed to be a certain way, individuals within that group sometimes feel trapped by that expectation, and end up giving in to it.

Antonio foresees his own doom by describing the necessary inflexibility of the law. Antonio seems resigned to his death, and what is most important to him is Bassanio. "—pray God Bassanio come / To see me pay his debt, and then I care not." Interestingly he does not discuss justice, but business, saying that the commercial welfare of Venice depends on these laws. "For the commodity that strangers have / With us in Venice, if it be denied, / Will much impeach the justice of his state." Here, we get a sense of both the instability and exciting possibilities that international business presents. Isn't this much like our current situation? People talk of world markets, "outsourcing," and huge corporate profits. There is a thrill and a worry. People want cheap products, but complain about everything being "made in China." There is a sense of patriotism for American-made goods, and a suspicion of foreigners and foreign goods. In this story, Shylock is an outsider, an "alien," working within Venice, contributing to its commercial life in his own way, yet he is despised for this.

ACT III, SCENE 4

OVERVIEW

At Portia's home, she and Lorenzo swap praises. He talks of her noble character and deeds and she replies that she does not turn away from good deeds. She talks of wanting to help when she can, and of how pleased she is to help Antonio, who, as Bassanio's friend, must be a great person. She says that one wants to spend time with people of high quality. She pulls back then, not wanting to brag, and lays out her false plan to leave her residence for quiet contemplation while Lorenzo and Jessica will be in charge of Belmont.

Next, Portia gives instructions to Balthazar, saying that he has always been trustworthy and she hopes he will continue to be so. He is to visit her cousin, Doctor Bellario, with her message and meet her in Venice with clothes and notes from him. She gives Nerissa hints of the plan that she has clearly already fully developed, but uses playful, tricky language, mentioning that they will see their husbands sooner than expected, that the husbands will see them but not know them. She talks of becoming men, and offers a bawdy caricature of what it means to be a man. Nerissa asks what this is all about, and Portia offers to fill her in offstage, allowing some suspense for the audience.

ANALYSIS

Who can you trust, what do surface appearances reveal, and who is really running the show? This scene raises all of these questions. While characters praise one another, Portia and Lorenzo, Portia for Balthazar, the emphasis on trust casts some doubt upon it. To automatically trust someone, and to say, "I can trust you, can't I?" are two different matters. The theme of judging others by the company they keep continues here, as Portia says any friend of Bassanio's is a friend of hers. She makes it clear that only the "right sort" should spend time together, which heightens Shylock's exclusion. Interestingly she talks of friends conversing and "wasting time" together. This could add to the view that she and her wealthy Venetian counterparts, especially Antonio, represent a corrupt or lazy nobility that lacks purpose and true convictions. When Portia asks that Balthazar waste no words, she brings out the theme of empty words and wise silence, or, in this case, words opposed to useful actions. She herself uses words cleverly. Some of Portia's speeches can be seen as empty or hypocritical, and the same can be said for most of the major characters. Portia doesn't just talk, though. She rushes to action, soon to be the most dramatic, plot-turning action in the play.

While Portia praises the men in this scene, in her mocking speech to Nerissa she talks of men as braggarts and liars. She, too, lies (behaving more like a man, or showing herself to be a hypocrite in her criticisms of men), saying the two women will wait in a monastery for their husbands, while actually planning to become a man and take action to save Antonio.

ACT III, SCENE 5

OVERVIEW

This light scene offers much play with words and establishes Jessica and Lorenzo as the temporary proprietors of Belmont. They do not have the status or grace of Portia and Bassanio, however, as shown in the circular, unserious language and in Launcelot's teasing of Jessica. He fears that she cannot avoid being damned, as the daughter of a Jew, and even being "saved" by her husband and converting is not a good thing, because one less Jew drives up the price of pork. Still, there is merriment and love, with talk of the upcoming meal and Jessica and Lorenzo's mutual admiration.

ANALYSIS

The most harshly anti-Semitic comments are hidden in comedy, which

TIM CARROLL DIRECTED THE ROYAL SHAKESPEARE COMPANY'S 2008 PRODUCTION FEATURING AMARA KARAN AS JESSICA AND PATRICK MOY AS LORENZO.

perhaps makes them less credible but nonetheless present. That Jessica can only be a stand-in mistress, a false and temporary one, clearly shows her lower status. Here, to be virtuous or "Christian'" is also to be a "bastard," meaning that her father is not her real father, which, of course, would speak badly of her mother, or else her father would be the wronged one. Notice, too, how this is reinforced by her praises for Portia, whom, she says, has no one equal. Indirectly she is putting herself down. Instead of immediately praising his new wife, Lorenzo instead assures her that he is Portia's equal. In a way, following the theme that our value comes from the company we keep, he is assuring her of her value or status, but at the same time, she does not get recognition here. When they joke about praises at the dinner table, the focus is still on her praising him instead of the other way around.

When Launcelot plays around with Lorenzo, he is intentionally misunderstanding a simple request to call people to dinner, but at the same time, showing his cleverness with language and the emptiness of such cleverness: "The fool hath planted in his memory / An army of good words, and I do know / A many fools that stand in better place, / Garnish'd like him, that for a tricksy word / Defy the matter." In a play where characters' hypocrisies are hinted at and critiqued, the fool or clown here reminds us to be suspicious of words, and to look below their surface.

ACT IV, SCENE 1

OVERVIEW

The duke and Antonio enter the Venetian courtroom with their attendants, discussing Shylock's angry inflexibility and Antonio's resignation. Antonio acknowledges the duke's good but unsuccessful efforts to dissuade his adversary. The duke then calls for Shylock. The duke tries one more time, saying to the moneylender that both he and everyone else expect Shylock to change his mind, to back down at the last minute, to show sympathy for Antonio and his unfortunate commercial losses, and not only not insist on the cruel bond, but forgive at least part of the loan. Shylock refuses. He says he has the legal right to claim the bond, and if this is not honored, the city's standing and freedom are at risk. He then addresses the cruelty and irrationality of his bond. He argues that he need not offer any reason at all, and has every right to follow his emotions, that people have irrational fear or hatreds, of rats, pigs or cats, so he can feel that way about Antonio.

Bassanio takes up the argument, saying that Shylock's reasons aren't good and asking why should he kill what he doesn't love. Shylock has no interest in pleasing Bassanio, retorting that no one would hate something and not want to kill it. Antonio, in his mood of resignation, tells Bassanio not to bother, that Shylock will not budge, and is in fact as unchangeable as nature: a wolf, the wind. Shylock reminds everyone that it is not even about money any more, and if he had six times the amount, he would still not back down. The duke introduces the idea of mercy, saying that Shylock can expect none if he offers none. Shylock says he is doing nothing wrong, that he is simply honoring the law, and he reminds all of those gathered that they buy slaves, thus exchanging human lives for money, and that he only purchased one pound of human flesh. To accept slavery means they must accept his action, or else their laws fall apart. The duke says he waits for Doctor Bellario, and Salerio mentions the arrival of a messenger. Bassanio tells Antonio not to lose hope, and that he would give up his own flesh and blood rather than let Antonio be harmed. Still Antonio feels lost, saying that Bassanio's best task now will be to write his epitaph.

The dramatic tension builds and builds, as Nerissa arrives, disguised as a young lawyer's assistant, and Shylock sharpens his knife. Bassanio and

DUSTIN HOFFMAN PLAYED SHYLOCK AT LONDON'S PHOENIX THEATER, 1989.

Gratiano talk to Shylock, criticizing him for his cruelty, which is harder and sharper than his knife. Like Antonio, Gratiano calls Shylock inhuman and wolflike. Shylock quips that Gratiano is wasting his breath, unless he can disprove the legality of the bond. Meanwhile, the duke receives Bellario's letter, which talks of his illness and the young lawyer (Portia in disguise) whom he recommends in his place.

Portia enters, asks for "the merchant" and "the Jew," and then affirms that Shylock does indeed have a legal right to claim his bond. Swiftly, though, she turns to him and says that he must be merciful. Shylock asks why he should. Portia then offers one of her most famous speeches, explaining the heavenly quality of mercy, a gift that is given yet grows, something that is godlike and separate from courtroom technicalities or earthly pettiness. Justice can't bring salvation, but mercy can. Shylock is still unmoved, insisting on the law. Portia asks about the loan, and Bassanio pleads with her to accept as much as ten times the original amount from him—anything to call off Shylock. Portia stays with the law, gaining Shylock's admiration and drawing out the agony and fear in all the others. She does try to offer Shylock three times the original amount, and he refuses. Portia tells Shylock to get ready to claim his bond, and perhaps baiting him while preparing for her final trick, asks that he not let Antonio bleed to death. Shylock points out that this detail is not stated directly in the bond. So, the bond must be taken literally, and soon this will be to Portia's advantage. But not yet. We all wait in suspense—most of all, Antonio, whom she now asks to speak. Antonio seems ready to die, saying that at least he can go before having to grow old and poor and saying that he truly loved Bassanio and has no regrets about dying for him.

Bassanio answers that, as much as he loves his wife, he would give her up and his own life, too, to save Antonio. Portia, in not a very lawyerly manner, chides Bassanio, saying that his wife, if she were here, would not like to hear that. Then Gratiano joins in, saying the same about Nerissa. In an aside Shylock says that he is the only one bothered by this, besides the wives, and says that if these are Christians, he would not want his daughter stuck with such people.

Portia moves on, saying that Shylock may now take his pound of flesh. At the last minute, she holds him off, and goes back to the wording of the bond. Since it only mentions flesh, not blood, he would have to take one without shedding a drop of the other. If he does so (which, of course, could not be avoided) he would lose all of his land and money to the state. She says, you wanted justice? Well, now you get it. Shylock goes back to the original offer of three times the loan, and Bassanio is ready to comply, but Portia won't have it. She says that Shylock must go through with the original claim, cutting the flesh, and shedding no blood, or else he dies and loses everything. Shylock wants to give up now, but there is more. Portia brings out another law, one about aliens intending to cause the death of a citizen. To comply with that law, Shylock must give half of his goods to the victim and half to the state.

The duke steps in and is the first to offer some mercy in this scene, saying that Shylock may keep his life and that the half due to the state may be commuted to a fine.

Shylock says that he might as well die. If his entire livelihood is taken away, he loses his life anyway.

Portia now asks Antonio about mercy. Antonio complies, saying that the half due to him should go instead to Lorenzo and Jessica, upon Shylock's death. There is one more stipulation: that Shylock convert to Christianity. The duke agrees that this is the only thing that would earn Shylock any leniency at this point. Shylock agrees, but immediately asks to be dismissed, as he is not well.

Now the others can celebrate. The duke invites Portia/the lawyer to dine with him, but she says she must go. Bassanio and Antonio praise and thank her, and offer to pay her for her services, but she declines. After some back and forth, she asks for a small token, the ring on Bassanio's finger. He tries to say no, but she acts insulted and Antonio urges him on, so he finally does part with it.

ANALYSIS

This is the climax of the play, where all of the themes unite in intense and suspenseful action. According to some, Shylock has gone mad with grief at the loss of his daughter. This is why his speech is repetitive, why he can't listen to others, why even money does not speak to him, only vengeance. When Shylock is urged to offer a gentle answer, his angry response shows his increasing madness, the fact that he is trapped by his own worst instincts. Notice how he says ". . . Must yield to such inevitable shame / As to offend, himself being offended," implying that what he has to do is shameful to himself. He wishes it were otherwise, but it is too late now. He also says that he follows a "losing suit." He probably foresees his own destruction, more like a tragic hero than a comic villain. The course has been set and he cannot stop it. He cannot be the simple greedy Jew caricature, or else he would have taken the money and run. His inflexibility is startling and cruel. But striking, too, is his isolation. He is alone in a Christian world, with a chorus of baiters and haters throughout the scene. Even the duke's request for a "gentle" response indicates this, with the pun on the word *Gentile* (meaning "non-Jewish"). The only way for him to be acceptable is to be Christian, and at the end, becoming a Christian is part of his punishment. The Christian view of mercy is thrust upon him. Portia as the lawyer says he "must" show mercy, but he is right to point out that in a court of law, there is no compulsion for such gestures. Later on, she is not able to offer what she had demanded of him. Once the flaw in the bond is pointed out, Bassanio is ready to offer Shylock the money and be done with it, but she won't stop at that. She forces his doom and humiliation.

The money theme runs throughout this exciting scene as well. Interestingly, in his sad dying speech, Antonio says that at least he can die young and wealthy instead of old and poor. Shylock, the supposedly money-obsessed character, will not be bought in this scene. Yet when his worldly goods are taken from him, he says that he may as well be dead. Bassanio offers bold, impulsive gifts to save his friend, which is similar to Antonio's generosity at the beginning of the play (although it is Portia's money with which he is being so generous).

Loyalty and friendship are also explored. Antonio is willing to die for his friend. Portia tests her new husband's loyalty with the ring, and he fails. The triangular situation is heightened when Antonio pretty much asks Bassanio to choose him over his wife (but he also includes the lawyer on his side, and this lawyer, of course, is actually Bassanio's wife): "Let his deservings and my love withal / Be valued 'gainst your wife's commandment." Shylock is friendless. His love for his daughter is displayed when he comments that she deserves a better husband than these Christians who forsake their wives for friends. Antonio is ready to die at the beginning of the scene, and keeps confirming this in each subsequent speech. Is this because the one he loves is taken? He is happier to die for Bassanio than continue living with him married to Portia. Or it could also be because he has lost the battle against his hate. This kind, generous merchant hates Shylock with the fierce, irrational, animal hate that Shylock feels for him, and he cannot live that way. Notice how he dehumanizes Shylock throughout the play, and here, when he compares Shylock to inhuman forces of nature, and Shylock does the same, when he compares his irrational loathing to the way others may feel about rats or pigs. In a way, Antonio can resolve his hate by offering Christian mercy and bringing Shylock (actually, forcing him) into his faith. To Shylock, however, this kind of inviting inclusion is painful, not celebratory.

ACT IV, SCENE 2

OVERVIEW

In this brief scene, Portia and Nerissa head toward Shylock's house, so he can sign the deed. Gratiano catches up with them to hand over Bassanio's ring. Portia asks that he thank him for her, and Nerissa suggests to Portia that she, too, will try to get the promised ring away from her husband. Portia confidently declares that they will outwit their husbands.

ANALYSIS

When Portia says, "That cannot be" to the dinner invitation, she may also be expressing dismay that her husband did actually give up the ring. Still she never loses her composure or is without a plan, and immediately is ready for the next stage of the plot of disguise and trickery, assuring Nerissa that they will "outface them, and outswear them too." Once again friendship is more reliable than love as Nerissa immediately agrees to follow her friend and mistress with the test of loyalty, risking the same disappointment in her own husband as Portia has just had to endure.

ACT V, SCENE 1

OVERVIEW

Lorenzo and Jessica enjoy the bucolic, romantic setting of Belmont, in stark contrast to the tense, gritty courtroom scene in Venice. They talk of love, but in a teasing way, mentioning famous pairs of lovers, but those known for difficult affairs with questions of loyalty. Lorenzo mentions Jessica in the third person, as if she is one from that list, and she adds that Lorenzo won Jessica with untrue vows of love. A messenger interrupts their playfulness to announce the arrival of Portia. Launcelot shows up and delivers a goofy version of the same message, that his master (Bassanio) is also on his way back. Lorenzo at first wants to rush in and get ready for their arrival, but then decides that they can enjoy the night a bit longer, and requests music to add to the lovely mood. He talks of the merits of music. Jessica says that music does not make her happy. Lorenzo goes on to discuss the taming and magical effects of music, and that a person who is not moved by music should not be trusted.

Portia and Nerissa arrive, note the music and how good it sounds at night, and then Lorenzo recognizes Portia's voice. She is told that Bassanio is also on his way back.

Then the husbands are there, and immediately after greeting one another, the wives ask about the rings, first Nerissa, and then Portia (after saying that her husband would never give it away). The women first say they will not enter their husband's beds until they see the rings, and then they reveal that they have the rings, but still don't give up the whole game, instead claiming that they have slept with the lawyer and his clerk (which of course they have, because they are these characters). As with the trial scene, there is long drawn-out suspense from intentional word play, but here the mood is light and teasing. Finally the women tell the whole story, and the amazed husbands are happy and hugely relieved. To add to the happiness, Antonio gets the news that his ships are actually fine, and Lorenzo and Jessica receive the news of their inheritance (from Shylock's penalty). The couples go off for the evening, and all is well, at least in Belmont.

ANALYSIS

Although this is the happy ending, the play is not a simple comedy. For a tidy wrap-up, Shylock would need to have been dispensed with lightly, either mocked as a completely ridiculous character, or turned around to the "good side." His sad departure from the courtroom and the ambivalent "goodness" of those who heckled and derided him do not offer this tidiness. The love, harmony, and music in the last act also are not pure or simple. The poetry that Lorenzo offers is indeed mellifluous and lovely, but he describes uncomfortable loves. When he includes Jessica in the list, he says, "In such a night / Did Jessica steal from the wealthy Jew, / And with an unthrift love did run from Venice," once again mixing money with love. The word *steal* can mean "sneak," as in "steal away," yet also, of course, it means taking money or goods from someone, which is what Jessica did to Shylock. They tease one another about not meaning their vows, and with the trick of the rings, loyalty again is being challenged. Jessica is not merry at the sound of music. This could make her untrustworthy, as Lorenzo says those who don't like music are, or it could show her unease at what she has done, her inability to rejoice completely.

Portia and Nerissa play at a mock infidelity, which is a light joke, yet still leaves us with that idea. These two certainly enjoy the music, and yet they, too, create or display a sense of unease when they comment that the setting or circumstances change things. The music is sweeter because it is night, and a nightingale singing at day would sound as harsh as a wren.

Portia is the witty trickster, the mistress of all the joy in Belmont. Antonio says to her, "Sweet lady, you have given me life and living; / For here I read for certain that my ships / Are safely come to road," and Lorenzo comments, "Fair ladies, you drop manna in the way / Of starved people." Money is really the hero here, though. Antonio's "life and living" are associated with his returned wealth, and Lorenzo's joy also comes from the same source. They all have won and Shylock has lost in terms of finances, and in one sense, that is what truly counts in this world.

LIST OF CHARACTERS

Antonio, the merchant

Bassanio, Antonio's best friend; in love with Portia

Portia, lady of Belmont; in love with Bassanio

Shylock, Jewish moneylender

Jessica, Shylock's daughter; in love with Lorenzo

Gratiano, a friend of Salerio, Antonio, and Lorenzo;
in love with Nerissa

Lorenzo, friend of Gratianio; in love with Jessica

Salerio, friend of Bassanio and Antonio

Solanio, friend of Bassanio and Antonio; with Salerio,
often serves as a go-between and messenger

The duke of Venice, judge in the courtroom

The prince of Morocco, first suitor of Portia

The prince of Arragon, second suitor of Portia

Tubal, a Jewish person and friend to Shylock

Nerissa, Portia's waiting-woman

Balthazar, Portia's servant

Launcelot Gobbo, servant to Shylock; later Bassanio's servant

Old Gobbo, Launcelot Gobbo's father

ANALYSIS OF MAJOR CHARACTERS

BASSANIO

Is he a lazy wastrel or a respectable aristocrat? The play begins with him already in debt to Antonio and yet taking on another loan. Apparently it was quite common in those days for aristocrats to be deeply in debt. When Nerissa and Portia first discuss him, Bassanio is described in admirable terms: "A Venetian, (a scholar and a soldier) . . . in company of the Marquis of Montferrat." Not only does he possess his own strong qualities, but he also keeps good company, which this society clearly values (as does ours). Antonio, his close friend, is often praised as being a worthy gentleman.

Bassanio is the lucky recipient of the two strongest loves in the story: from Antonio and Portia. We do not see a lot of what he does or why he deserves this, and this ambiguity adds to Shakespeare's themes about money and appearance versus reality. Do we judge people too much based on what they have, how they appear, and who they spend time with? Bassanio also represents the importance of love and friendship. Antonio seems to gain his sense of purpose and source of greatness from the sacrifice he is willing to make for Bassanio. Portia is rescued from the tedious and frightening casket game by the one she really does love, Bassanio. Perhaps his strength or merit is in seeing past surfaces and recognizing the true friend and the true lover. He chooses to trust Antonio and he chooses the lead casket, the least flashy, the one with the inscription asking him to give of himself, not congratulating him for what he is or what he deserves.

Even this is not simple, however. Shakespeare never makes it easy, because life is not easy. When Bassanio chooses that lead casket, he appears virtuous, and yet the inscription is highly ironic. "Who chooseth me must give and hazard all he hath," but what has Bassanio given up thus far? He has taken, not given—taken a loan from Antonio that puts his dear friend's life at risk, and he has used this money to woo Portia, who gives him all of herself and her incredible wealth as soon as he passes the test. In a way, then, Bassanio is actually the gold casket; he does gain what all men desire. In another complication, Bassanio cannot love both Antonio and Portia, especially if one sees the homosexual component in Antonio's attachment to his dear friend. In the trial scene, Bassanio chooses Antonio over Portia, when he says he would choose his life over hers. This is, of course, in the heat of the moment when it appears that Antonio might be losing his life. Portia pushes the point further when, disguised as the lawyer, she cajoles Bassanio into handing over the wedding ring she had given him. In this sense, Bassanio does not seem worthy of Portia's love. All sorts of references to disloyalty and instability in relationships run throughout the play, especially toward the end, yet we are still given the happy ending. After teasing their husbands and giving them quite a scare, Portia and Nerissa make up with them. Perhaps, then, Bassanio represents both the challenge and value of loving relationships.

PORTIA

This lovely, virtuous woman lives in posh Belmont, with old, secure money. She is desirable to all suitors, and Belmont is the place to be, free of the commercial chaos found in Venice. Like Antonio, she is in a position where she can afford to be generous to friends, even helping Antonio, who is her lover's friend. Portia remains loyal to her father, by carrying out his decree with the three caskets, but she does so grudgingly. She does not seem to trust fate or her father entirely, yet her compliance is rewarded when Bassanio, her first choice, wins the prize: Portia herself.

In one sense, Portia is passive, almost symbolic. She represents mercy, heaven, and "Christian virtues." She waits in Belmont for suitors to arrive. She likes Bassanio, but must sit patiently through each visitor's attempts at the casket, and submit to whomever wins. Belmont is the paradise where, once you get there, everything seems to work itself out, as happens at the end. Yet women are never merely submissive or subdued for Shakespeare. When Bassanio is put to the casket test, Portia sings that little song with the rhymes, perhaps as background confirmation of Bassanio's cleverness and virtue, or perhaps offering him a little sneaky clue. She can be admired for her ability to use language and disguise not only to win the day for the heroes, but also to challenge the restrictive roles of women. As a male lawyer, she displays great cleverness as she redefines the terms of the bond. She also plays with language and toys with her new husband in the ploy with the ring. The ring is typically given by the man, the terms set by him, but in this play, it is the women who do so. The shape itself could represent her genitals, as shown in the very last line of the play, with Gratiano's joke about keeping Nerissa's ring safe. Portia and Nerissa give their husbands a scare, talking of sleeping with the lawyer and his clerk, respectively. Not only do they force the issue of infidelity, showing that they have something to say about it, but they equate themselves with men, claiming the power, intelligence, and freedom of movement associated with men. "The ring comes to mean female self-expression, female sexuality, changeability and unruliness. The symbol of male possession of women is transformed into a symbol of women slipping out of male power."

Does Portia go too far with her cleverness, though? She is an actress, and she seems more excited about her disguise than about actually saving Antonio. She draws out the tension in the trial scene like a master dramatist, waiting until Shylock's knife is poised and Antonio is sure of his own death before pulling out the interpretation of the bond that will save Antonio's life.

She also does this in the last act, yet the tone is light and sexy, as she and Nerissa lead their husbands quite far in their fears of their wives' infidelity, before finally sharing the trick. Because she cannot offer the mercy to Shylock that she asks of him, and because of her enjoyment of show over content, perhaps she herself, like Bassanio, is the golden casket. To be fair to Portia, however, she does the best she can in an unfair, uncomfortable world, where lovers cannot be trusted and women's lives are limited. Even in the trial scene, she may be enjoying the show to a degree, but maybe she is also making it up as she goes along, and only at the last minute is she able to figure out how to save Antonio. She is not a lawyer by training, after all. She has money, yes, but otherwise, she has more restrictions than freedom, and yet she manages to build a life for herself that she can be happy with, and she makes all those around her happy, too.

ANTONIO

The play is named after this character, and yet he remains quite vague. He is wealthy and respectable, courageous and generous in offering the dangerous bond for his friend, and then coming so close to losing his life over it; yet he also keeps the religious strife and animosity with Shylock going. In the first scene where they meet, he states that friendship is impossible. Shylock mentions his spitting on him and otherwise shunning him over the years. Then, in the trial scene, Antonio says it is useless trying to reason with Shylock, with his hard, Jewish heart.

Is Antonio's intense love for Bassanio romantic? He has no female love interest in the play, and in the trial scene, he expresses deep love for Bassanio. A historical note here: Although homosexuality has been around from the beginning of time, it is believed that only in the past hundred years or so have people associated sexual orientation with personal identity. In Elizabethan times, one might woo and marry someone of the opposite sex, and secretly engage in homosexual activity. It was not considered odd for a man to love another man, yet sex between them was considered a sin, and therefore kept secret. This was not uncommon, and there has been speculation about Shakespeare himself having homosexual relationships.

Harold C. Goddard notes that Antonio's mysterious sadness cannot be completely attributed to jealousy over Bassanio's pursuit of Portia, because most of that story comes after the sadness is mentioned. He asserts that what is plaguing Antonio most is his indescribable, uncontrollable hatred of Shylock, which actually stems from recognizing himself in his enemy. When someone—our parents, siblings, or good friends—somehow reminds us of what we like least about ourselves, a natural impulse is to hate them or push them away somehow. Interestingly, this play's title early on was posted as either *The Merchant of Venice* or *The Jew of Venice*, a clue about this parallel between the two main characters. Notice, too, Portia's line during the trial scene: "Which is the merchant here and which the Jew?" The simple meaning, of course, is just that as a lawyer, she wants to identify the defendant and the plaintiff, but the other meaning does indicate that these two are, on some level, interchangeable. Each talks of the other as an animal. Neither can back down from hateful language and behavior, even when others are willing to make amends. Both make money from money. The discomfort in Shakespeare's day with usury also affected views of capitalism in general, of making something from nothing, which was considered unnatural, against God in a way. In the scene when Shylock refers to Jacob and the loan of sheep and Antonio gets impatient, not seeing the connection to the issue of interest, he asks, "And what of him? Did he take interest?" Shylock replies, "No, not take interest; not, as you would say, / Directly interest." As already mentioned, this could be Shylock's way of setting the stage for his very creative suggestion for the bond, but it could also be a highly sarcastic line, where he hints that Antonio gains interest, too, just in a different form. Antonio represents the "good Christian" in opposition to Shylock "the Jew," and yet his hateful, "un-Christian" behavior challenges the validity of these simple generalizations.

Perhaps Antonio is the quintessential gambler, and is uneasy at the beginning of the play because he has nothing to lose. He is a self-made man who is too successful. When Shylock offers him the crazy bond, he finally has a challenge to spark his interest. Even knowing that he may lose Bassanio or his own life, Antonio agrees. Tony Church, who played the role of Antonio with the Royal Shakespeare Company, says, "Have you ever met a gambler? Antonio offers his flesh as surety because Shylock challenges him to gamble. Shylock suddenly challenges Antonio to a stupid dare that Shylock will definitely lose, but he does it to make Antonio the laughingstock of the Exchange. Shylock essentially says, Put your life on the line. That appeals to Antonio, since it's the only thing left he hasn't gambled. It has all the romantic appeal of the ultimate risk."

Goddard asserts that Antonio is the silver casket: "He got as much as he deserved; material success and a suicidal melancholy."

SHYLOCK

This character steals the show, even though he is only present in five of the play's twenty scenes. He is a fascinating, powerful, complex, and highly controversial figure. His name has become a cliché, and many who never saw or read the play know the name. At this level, the associations are not positive. The mythology of the greedy usurer Jew preceded *The Merchant of Venice*, but ironically, because of the realism and power of this character, the myth was kept alive by and associated with Shylock's name. At first, Shylock was played as a simple villain, with a devilish red wig and all. This was done all the way through the late nineteenth century. In the late twentieth century, he began to be played as the long-suffering Jew. Today the subtleties and ambiguities of this character are heightened.

Shylock does love his money, but for him, wealth does not come or stay easily. Because of prejudices and the social and legal limitations to his success, he does not have the luxury of being generous to debtors. Since money is his only source of power and respect, he must hold on to it at all costs. He is described throughout the play as greedy and vengeful. He is equated with the devil. Clearly Christianity is the favored faith, and the "happy ending" confirms this, with Jessica choosing it and Shylock being forced into it. His Christian enemies, however, are perhaps equally corrupt, maybe even more trivial and vapid than he, for the loss of his daughter offers strong motivation for his vengeance, while they are given no such motivation. He does turn down money, too, in the trial scene. When he is offered twice the amount of the original loan, he refuses it and demands the bond. Although this vengeance seems unnecessarily brutal, he still gains sympathy. Everyone is against him in the trial scene. At the end of this scene, when Shylock says simply and quietly that he is not well, he becomes a sad, not a hateful, character. He could have stalked off angrily, or given in cheerfully, marking his conversion to Christianity as the happy ending it may appear to be. But he is pained instead, bringing out the bullying tone of the Christians surrounding him, from Portia and her merciless refusal to back down from the most extreme punishment, to the jeering crowd and Antonio's gang.

David Suchet, an associate artist of the Royal Shakespeare Company who played Shylock in 1981, has this to say about the character: "I disagree with every critic who says it is an anti-Semitic play. Shakespeare would never have done that—not with Marlowe's play *The Jew of Malta* playing down the road, which is very anti-Semitic . . . . And Shylock is redeemed at the end of the play."

In one interpretation, Shylock is mainly a lonely old miser. His beloved wife is dead, he is estranged from his daughter, and he is excluded from most of Venetian society. His most intimate relationship is with Antonio, his enemy. He might keep that feud going partly as a way of having some kind of connection with another person.

Since the play is as much about money as religion, if not more so, Shylock's character throws into relief the flaws and hypocrisies of his Christian counterparts. They focus on ships and fancy clothes more than on God. People are valued for their money: Bassanio, Antonio, Portia. They rebuke Shylock for his need for vengeance, yet they behave in the same way. Shylock points out that they keep slaves while he only goes after one man, Antonio. They refer to Christian virtues that they don't all uphold. Are his flaws—his vengeful pursuit and his focus on money—signs of the times, associated with his race, or are they individual qualities? Shakespeare raises, but does not answer, this question.

Shylock seems to become more and more confused and enraged as the play develops, perhaps pushed toward madness by circumstances. This could mean that he does not have a careful, evil plot that he sits back smugly and enjoys. If so, he becomes a complex, compelling character. He at least has the potential for nobility. He does not actually behave as the purely avaricious Jew. He will not take twice the amount of the loan during the trial. When he hears of the futility of his efforts to find Jessica, he says he wishes she were dead and buried with the jewels, not that he had those jewels; he is struggling with his miserliness, and wishing it gone and buried. He is misunderstood and not appreciated. This could indicate that Shylock is the lead casket.

A CLOSER LOOK

- THEMES

- MOTIFS

- SYMBOLS

- LANGUAGE

- INTERPRETING THE PLAY

Jeremy Irons, Al Pacino, and ▶
Joseph Fiennes starred in a
2004 film adaptation of the play.

AL
PACINO

JEREMY
IRONS

JOSEPH
FIENNES

LYNN
COLLINS

WILLIAM
SHAKESPEARE'S *Der*
KAUFMANN von
VENEDIG

CHAPTER
THREE

a Closer Look

THEMES

THE TESTING OF LOYALTY

The ring story is a source of humor and playfulness, but it also brings out one of the play's themes: how loyalty is defined and tested. Portia and Nerissa approve their husbands with the rings they offer, elicit promises about them, and then, in their alter egos of lawyer and lawyer's clerk, pressure the husbands into breaking these promises. They go so far as to claim infidelity later on. Portia announces that she invited the lawyer to her bed, which is true, of course, because she *is* the lawyer. Nerissa does the same. While the husbands fail the test and the wives toy with them to an extreme degree, all is forgiven and laughed off. The more serious betrayal over a ring is when Jessica makes a mockery of the ring she took from her father, a gift from his deceased wife. Jessica ends up swapping it for a monkey while she is on her escapades with Lorenzo, and Shylock hears word of this. In a sense, loyalty and promises are taken lightly among the Christians, but they weigh heavily in the Jewish family. Still there is the loyalty between Antonio and Bassanio, which is very intense indeed, and leads to speculation of a homosexual component to their relationship. In the same packed scene where Portia plays the lawyer and the loyalty over the rings is tested, Bassanio asserts that his own life and his love for his wife are not worth the life of Antonio. Of course, this is a highly charged moment, when Antonio seems on the verge of losing his life, but it nonetheless points out the very strong bond between these two men. The audience or reader is left to ponder this theme. Is the friendship between Antonio and Bassanio admirable or are expectations too high? Can you ever completely trust a friend or romantic partner, and should that trust be tested?

THE EFFECTS OF MONEY

Another theme looks at how money affects our judgment of and interactions with others. Money is central to *The Merchant of Venice*. Bassanio doesn't have enough. He has to borrow some in order to feel worthy of Portia, and he uses it to woo her. Portia is equated with monetary value when her suitors need to choose a gold, silver, or lead casket in order to win her. Is people's worth measured by their wealth? Do people foolishly judge others simply by the surface? Think about a

HE IS WELL PAID THAT IS WELL SATISFIED.

cute guy or girl whom you notice driving a fancy car or wearing beautiful (expensive) clothes. Do those outward trappings of wealth make the person more appealing to you? In *Merchant*, greed is a source of pain and disappointment. This clearly involves more than just the character of Shylock. According to some readers, he actually is most sympathetic, because his own daughter betrays him. In the trial scene, when Shylock is offered three times the amount of money due him, he declines, demonstrating that he values more than money.

Says David Suchet of the Royal Shakespeare Company,

> PORTIA IS A TOTALLY CONFUSED, MONEY-GOVERNED PERSON, DESPERATELY WISHING TO FIND HUMAN VALUES. THE WHOLE PLAY HAS TO DO WITH MONEY, NOT RACISM. SHYLOCK COMES ON AND HIS FIRST LINE IS "THREE THOUSAND DUCATS, WELL." EVERYBODY WANTS TO MARRY PORTIA BECAUSE SHE IS SO WEALTHY. SHE HAS TO FIND LOVE IN THE PLAY. THAT'S WHAT SHAKESPEARE IS SAYING THROUGHOUT *MERCHANT*: THE REAL VALUE IS IN PEOPLE, NOT MONEY.

In a way, money fuels the whole play, which is a circle of exchanges. The same amount that Bassanio borrows from Antonio, thus binding Antonio to Shylock, is what Bassanio uses to woo Portia, and once he wins her, she is the one who comes to the rescue and severs the connection between Antonio and Shylock. Shylock tries to claim ownership of Antonio's flesh, parallel to the way his Christian neighbors own slaves. The marriage bond also represents ownership. Value is translated across disguises, too, with Portia and Nerissa most powerful when they are men. Personal rights and property rights are inextricably connected. Shylock says, "You take my life / When you do take the means whereby I live," and Antonio makes similar connections between livelihood, or money, and life. The play could be an indictment of the ugliness of capitalism and its effects on people and their relationships. And yet there is also the struggle of genuine feelings, friendship, and love fighting against this or even complementing it. The Renaissance suspicion of usury has deep philosophical and religious origins. Aristotle talked about the unnaturalness of something coming from nothing, saying that this is against nature and against God. Money, or metal, cannot reproduce. That's for people to do. But poetry is making something from nothing. There are exchanges that can magically lead to increase. Even homosexual love (deemed "unnatural" because it cannot lead to a baby) does create love, and increase in that sense. Taking interest, then, is part of this continuum of magic for Shakespeare, and to take it one step further, as Frederick Turner does, *Merchant* is actually an acceptance of capitalism, its merits and complexities. Once again, this theme can be taken in several directions, and Shakespeare leaves much open to individual interpretation. A stage or film director has a lot of room to play with, but clearly the play looks at how money binds us to one another and influences our judgments.

APPEARANCE VERSUS REALITY

The central, unifying theme is appearance versus reality. You find this with the casket story, as a component of the money theme, and even in the inner conflicts of Shakespeare's characters. The surfaces of the caskets do not indicate what is inside, and it takes wisdom to see past the shining gold, sleek silver, and dull lead. Money can be misleading, too. Having it makes one alluring and appealing, like Portia, and yet it isn't the money that brings these characters—or us—happiness. Antonio is most happy when he gives his money away. Shylock's attachment to his money makes him miserable, and Portia falls in love with a man who is in debt. There is also a contrast or conflict between the conscious and subconscious. One could argue that this is even present in Shakespeare's own genius.

Let's take a look at Shylock, probably the most complex and fascinating character. We struggle with our assessment of him: Is he a comical

"ALL THAT GLISTERS IS NOT GOLD."

caricature? Is he sympathetic? Does he love money too much? Does he love his daughter? But why can't it be all of the above? He himself struggles with these issues. Do any of us have one and only one trait? When he first negotiates the bond with Antonio, he may in part genuinely want to be Antonio's friend, to be able to set aside racial and commercial animosities. He speaks of friendship and offers a loan without interest, which is very unlike his usual practice. Perhaps he is testing Antonio, "killing him with kindness," and Antonio fails that test. Antonio says, we're enemies, I'll keep spitting on you, just give me the loan the way you would any of your enemies. Later, when Shylock is quoted as crying, "My daughter! My ducats!" these could be the words of a comical miser, or else a confused old man who truly loves his daughter but also loves his money. In any of the heated moments, when Shylock's words are vengeful and hateful (Antonio's, too, for that matter), the drama of the scene, the pressure from those around him, all of this forces one side of the personality to express itself. Think of a time when you blurted something out, or acted impulsively in an emotional moment, and then seconds later, thought, "Oh no! I can't believe I just said or did that!" Well, you're not alone. Shakespeare is right there with you.

Along these lines, if we look again at Shylock as a mirror to the other characters and their flaws, they hate and scapegoat him because they do not want to face these qualities in themselves. Harold Goddard puts this succinctly:

MOTIFS

Racial conflict is a motif that pushes the dramatic tension and heightens the play's themes. Perhaps Shakespeare understood quite well the perspective of a member of an oppressed group. If Antonio or Bassanio misbehaved, they would be criticized as individuals, but if Shylock missteps, he is judged as the representative of his entire race. Think about how racism operates today. A famous person who happens to belong to a minority group behaves in a shocking or dramatic manner, and people tend to make assumptions about that person's ethnic group, instead of him as an individual, whereas if a member of the majority behaved the same way, it is less likely that there would be judgments and statements about how "*those* people are." If this is so in this play, then Shylock's vengeance too is for all Jews. "Thou call'dst me dog before thou hadst a cause, / But since I am a dog, beware my fangs." Perhaps Shylock's only source of power and respect is through money, which is why he hates Antonio so for lending it free of interest, while Antonio, given his social status, can afford to be generous.

The endless cycle of generalizing or stereotyping is set in motion, so

Shylock comments during the trial scene that he would hate the idea of his daughter marrying such "Christian husbands" as Antonio and Bassanio, who claim their friendship to be greater than their bonds with their wives. And then, of course, the "happy ending" has Shylock forced to convert to Christianity, as Jessica has done, and will all of his fortune to her and her new Christian husband. To the Venetians, "Christian" is good and "Jewish" is bad, but the play's tensions and ambiguities question this, showing the pain and loss associated with such hateful generalizations. It is not completely clear how much the generalizations are included simply to please Shakespeare's audience by reflecting prejudices, and how much he is presenting a situation for analysis and critique of his society's flawed thinking (and ours).

Setting serves as a motif, bringing out themes quite starkly in this play, with Venice representing the uneasiness, chaos, and brutality of commerce and capitalism, while peaceful Belmont is the placid site of old money and values. Venice is a man's world. Even when Portia and Nerissa visit, they are disguised as men; the objects found there are moneybags and Shylock's knife, while Belmont is a woman's world, with men coming only as wooers and suitors. The props associated with this moonlit location are connected with women and fairy tales: rings, caskets, and music. Belmont is where everyone wants to go, and only the "villain," Shylock, does not make it there. Antonio, his nemesis, goes there briefly, and yet remains aloof and unattached. One way of looking at this is that neither of these characters is freed from his hate, and so they cannot fully enter the paradise of Belmont. This is where the happy ending is delivered, and Portia is the one who offers it, in the form of the joking reconciliation between her and Nerissa with their husbands, the good news for Lorenzo and Jessica about inheriting Shylock's money, and the good news for Antonio about his successful ships. Lorenzo rejoices, saying, "Fair ladies, you drop manna in the way / Of starved people." Portia, the angel from paradise, enters the dirty world of Venice in order to restore peace and save Antonio. Is she tainted by this world, or never fully the angel that she seems to be? As with everything else for Shakespeare, the distinctions between these two settings and what they represent are not clear-cut. Jessica seems not fully welcome in blissful Belmont. Portia is not fully kind or merciful in the trial scene, and of course Shylock is not fully bad or Antonio fully good. Money itself and its powers are not completely dirty or negative. Venice comes to Belmont and Belmont to Venice. We are never separate from our basest instincts or our heavenly goodness.

SYMBOLS

The physical representation of the theme appearance versus reality is alchemy: one substance changing into another. Lead is gold, gold is lead. What you see is not what you get. There is the worldly and the spiritual, and one must not be confused with the other. Characters are put to the test of recognizing the truth beneath the surface, and most fail. Some may succeed in one sense, as Bassanio sees through the surface of the caskets and picks the right one, and perhaps Portia recognizes true greatness in him. Yet as discussed earlier, Bassanio is not completely admirable, nor is Portia. She fails the test in the trial scene. We readers and audience members are put to this test, too, as we try to assess each character and the play. We are tested daily as well, in our interactions with friends, family, colleagues, and supposed enemies. Alchemy is also magic, though, and perhaps resolves conflicts. Usury was seen as suspect because metal does not create, so interest on investments seems unnatural. Yet in this play, metal or money is equated with life, with flesh, and it transforms life. Both Shylock and Antonio talk of their money as being equivalent to their lives. The wedding rings represent wedding vows (and Bassanio says he would cut off his left hand defending the ring) and the female body. As stated above, money is, in a way, the hero that fixes everything, at least on a superficial level (but its allures and surface appeal are dangerous, too). Another way of looking at it is that money itself is not good or bad. How people use it and give it value determines its goodness or evil.

Depending on a person's interpretation of the play, the characters themselves are symbols: Shylock could symbolize greed or exclusion or racial scapegoating. He could also be the lead casket, as stated earlier. Portia could symbolize grace, wealth, and mercy, or hypocrisy. She could be the gold casket. Bassanio, too, paired with her, could be the symbol of trueness in friendship and love, or also shallow surface gleam, the gold casket. Antonio could represent "Christian" self-sacrifice and goodness, except for his hatred of Shylock and his general, ill-defined malaise. This makes him the silver casket, getting what he deserves.

If the symbolism seems fuzzy and nebulous, that is understandable, and that is part of what Shakespeare is trying to say. It is our need to summarize and judge quickly and simply that gets us into trouble, fitting people into little boxes (caskets?) and interpreting circumstances or relationships in a one-dimensional manner.

LANGUAGE

Norman N. Holland looks closely at how different the two settings, Venice and Belmont, are, even in terms of the language used in each. As has already been pointed out, Venice represents harsh, determined commercialism, while Belmont represents a fairy-tale paradise. In Venice, the characters talk about money and investments, while in Belmont, they refer to mythology and fairy tales. In Belmont, all is love, harmony and music. Lorenzo and Jessica share their loving exchanges, referring to legendary lovers such as Troilus and Cressida and Pyramus and Thisbe. They also talk of the calming, celebratory effects of music. This contrasts with Shylock back in Venice, who has no interest in the masque and warns Jessica to close the windows against the noise.

> WHAT, ARE THERE MASQUES? HEAR YOU ME, JESSICA:
> LOCK UP MY DOORS; AND WHEN YOU HEAR THE DRUM
> AND THE VILE SQUEALING OF THE WRY-NECKED FIFE,
> CLAMBER NOT YOU UP TO THE CASEMENTS THEN, . . .
> BUT STOP MY HOUSE'S EARS I MEAN MY CASEMENTS;
> LET NOT THE SOUND OF SHALLOW FOPP'RY ENTER
> MY SOBER HOUSE.

In Venice, there is worry and scarcity. Solanio and Salerio talk of the merchant's worried frame of mind: ". . . every object that might make me fear / Misfortune to my ventures, out of doubt / Would make me sad." While in Belmont, there is excess and growth: ". . . yet for you / I would be trebled twenty times myself, / A thousand times more fair, ten thousand times more rich. . . ." Portia brings this world of plenty to Venice when she enters the courtroom and asks that Shylock give mercy: "It is twice blest; / It blesseth him that gives and him that takes."

F. E. Halliday is not fond of the play, but he finds the language praiseworthy: "It is the last of the great series of lyrical dramas, and at the same time the first of the sequence of comedies in which prose is as important a medium as verse." The use of assonance and internal rhyme in this play is highly successful, from the opening speeches of the first act to some of the more famous speeches, such as Portia's on mercy. Shylock, on the other hand, is associated with prose. He moves the drama forward, forcing characters to respond to him, not the audience. This play can be studied in terms of Shakespeare's developing skills. In earlier plays, prose serves the plot and poetry is a divergence, often offering the playwright direct input on important themes. Later in this play, however, poetic language is also used in taut, plot-pushing moments, such as when a servant announces Bassanio's arrival to Belmont in sonnetlike language. "A day in April never came so sweet, / To show how costly summer was at hand...." Act III, Scene 1 shows the first time a major character (Shylock) speaks only serious, dramatic prose. This mixed use of prose and verse is considered more sophisticated than what is found in Shakespeare's earlier plays, and leads toward the plays that follow. Shylock speaks with repetitive rhythms as found in the Psalms, so this is prose very close to verse, very strong and evocative, but it is prose nonetheless. The trial scene, too, offers focused drama with all skilled uses of language furthering the story, not diverging from it. Halliday and others do not find the language in this scene to be Shakespeare's best, noting in particular Portia's often-quoted speech on mercy. This could also mark the play as transitional, in terms of Shakespeare's expertise. It is in the final act, when Shylock is done with, that the pure poetry of music, love, and harmony can take over.

AS A PLAY, *THE MERCHANT OF VENICE* IS BOTH MADE AND MARRED BY SHYLOCK; HE IS HIMSELF ONE OF THE TRIUMPHS OF SHAKESPEARE'S DRAMATIC GENIUS, AND AT THE SAME TIME A MAIN CAUSE OF ITS SUDDEN DEVELOPMENT; HE TAUGHT SHAKESPEARE A DRAMATIC LANGUAGE. ON THE OTHER HAND, SIMPLY BECAUSE HE IS WHAT HE IS, HE LAYS BARE THE BASER QUALITIES OF THE OTHER CHARACTERS, THE SELFISHNESS, INSINCERITY, BRUTALITY, THAT ARE ONLY SKINNED AND FILMED BY THEIR VIRTUES.... BUT AS POETRY THE PLAY IS BEYOND REPROACH.

Still Shakespeare does not give language obvious value or status. The theme of appearance versus reality (or lead versus gold) applies to language as well. Characters often mock themselves or others for talking too much and speaking empty words, or comment that wisdom is often hidden in silence, masked by words. Gratiano shows this in the first scene when trying to cheer up Antonio, and Launcelot Gobbo is a caricature of vapid, seemingly meaningless chatter.

G. R. Hibbard notes that while prose and verse mark the lowest to the highest status in characters, from Launcelot Gobbo on the one end of the continuum to the duke on the other, at the same time, with the Shylock–Antonio opposition or the money versus love conflict, there aren't clear or obvious distinctions. Instead he observes that the whole play is about trials: Antonio's friendship with Bassanio is tried or tested; Bassanio's love for Portia is on trial with the trick of the rings; there is the literal trial, of course, with Shylock and Antonio; and Portia's loyalty to her father is tested by means of the casket riddles. In both prose and verse, the mode of communication is argumentative. Logic is used to justify choices. Launcelot's speech mocks this in Act II, Scene 2, when he says that while we refer to logic, it is actually pleasure and convenience that dictate our decisions. "My conscience is but a kind of hard conscience to offer to counsel me to stay with the Jew. The fiend gives the more friendly counsel. I will run, fiend; my heels are at your commandment; I will run."

Antonio is the only character who speaks entirely in verse. He also shares his feelings directly, which puts him in a vulnerable position. The only time when he uses this language of argument is in his very hateful speech during the trial, when he compares Shylock to uncontrollable features of nature, saying that he would be as impossible to change as these. Antonio and Shylock are opponents and opposites. Shylock's language is guarded and careful, even though his emotions are clearly just as powerful as Antonio's. Shylock uses repetition and calculation.

SHYLOCK: THREE THOUSAND DUCATS WELL.
BASSANIO: AY, SIR, FOR THREE MONTHS.
SHYLOCK: FOR THREE MONTHS WELL.
BASSANIO: FOR THE WHICH, AS I TOLD YOU,
ANTONIO SHALL BE BOUND.
SHYLOCK: ANTONIO SHALL BECOME BOUND WELL.

This same pattern of building up an argument and using repetition, like that of a debater or politician, comes forth passionately and dramatically in Shylock's "Hath not a Jew eyes" speech. Shylock, though, is ever practical, and his speech moves away from figurative into the literal, for example, "land-rats and water-rats, water-thieves and land thieves . . . I mean pirates" or "stop my house's ears—I mean my casements." Shylock's calculating, cautious style puts him in a powerful position. This shows in the scene when the bond is first set and Antonio is the one who loses his composure: "Why, look you, how you storm!" It carries all the way through the trial scene, when he uses repetition to insist on the legality of the bond. Here, he uses a question and answer argument when he explains why he is insisting on this: "You'll ask me why I rather choose to have / A weight of carrion flesh than to receive / Three thousand ducats." Although they are opposites, Shylock and Antonio's animosity is also the same, in that each sees the other as animal, not human. Shylock's strength and coolness are turned against him in mockery when he loses the trial and slinks from the room, utterly defeated. Still his power is felt. As the character with perhaps the most dramatic and effective speeches, once he is gone from the play, the conversation of love, jokes about the rings, and other discussions appear as trivial chatter. The weight of Shylock and what he represents is not lost. In the spirit of a romantic comedy, the play closes in Belmont, with all sorts of happy resolutions, and yet there are references to infidelity, and the character who has the last word, Gratiano, is not a particularly appealing one. "As he has already gloated over Shylock's downfall, so he now dwells greasily in anticipation of the night he is about to spend with Nerissa. To regard the ending as happy or as a satisfactory solution is to approve of Gratiano, which is, I find, quite impossible." Shakespeare never glosses over truths. The arguments are not finished.

INTERPRETING THE PLAY

The Merchant of Venice is a messy play in that it combines three found stories, seems to be not quite a comedy, and presents controversial topics in highly ambiguous ways. Some critics find it imperfect for these reasons, an experiment that did not quite succeed. (See Elmer Edgar Stoll's "*The Merchant of Venice* Is a Comedy"; D. A. Traversi's "*The Merchant of Venice*: An Imperfect Step Toward Later Comedies"; or Gareth Lloyd Evans's "*The Merchant of Venice* Lacks Dramatic Unity.") Just because Shakespeare is very famous and brilliant, there is no reason not to find flaws in his work.

Literary criticism of the work seems to follow two main trends: one that looks at it in terms of fairy tale and allegory, and the other that looks at the realism of it through the lens of psychoanalytical (mainly Freudian), feminist, or other modern theories. According to Craig Bernthal, those who miss the allegorical element are unwilling to accept the play in its historical context, and force modern interpretations on it that are not appropriate, including labeling it as sexist, anti-Semitic, or heterosexist. Bernthal mentions another notable critic in his camp, Barbara Kiefer Lewalski.

Perhaps this need not be an either/or option. Following the first approach, one would appreciate the pound of flesh story as allegorical and not to be taken literally. (And, in one sense, Shylock fails when he tries to force the merry bond into a literal interpretation.) Portia and her caskets represent an old tale of the princess and the three princes—always three—and always the third wins. But Freudian interpretations also look to tropes or cultural motifs. This same princess story (also in King Lear, the story of the judgment of Paris, and Cinderella) is interpreted along these lines as representing man's movement toward death. The princess in her youth and beauty actually represents the opposite: death, but also "Mother Earth," to whom we all return. The Freudian and the allegorical approaches do seem to agree when it comes to the religious symbolism. Antonio is like Jesus, saintly, giving to those in need, sacrificing himself and his own body, angry at the "money changers," representing merciful judgment. Shylock represents Old Testament, rigid, rule-based justice, corrupt moneylending, and unbending cruelty. Although Antonio is not particularly kind or accepting of Shylock throughout the play, which does seem to challenge this view, he does show mercy at the end, when he suggests that the half of Shylock's penalty meant for Antonio be given back to Shylock. In a sense, "saving his soul" by requiring Shylock's conversion to Christianity could also be seen as merciful, if the perspective is one from a strongly Christian world.

Staying with the religious interpretation, Belmont ("beautiful mountain") represents heaven, where those who sacrifice are rewarded. The plot represents an allegorical journey toward spiritual life or death. Commercial, corrupt Venice threatens the spiritual life, but those who can eschew dirty money obsessions gain access to Belmont, heaven, the spiritual life. (Of course, ironically, Portia has no need to worry about money or trouble herself with the business of acquiring wealth.) Portia says she "stands for sacrifice." Bassanio chooses the casket with the inscription that mentions giving, not receiving. Jessica runs away from her moneylending father. Lorenzo exclaims, "Fair ladies, you drop manna in the way / Of starved people," referring to heavenly communion. All who enter Belmont have left Venice both physically and symbolically.

Directors and actors of course interpret the play, too, not just literary critics. The way this story has been played or filmed offers additional, perhaps more immediate, interpretations. Shylock was played as the simple villain for years. There were exceptions, but post-Holocaust versions became more difficult. One turning point was Michael Langham's production in 1960 at Stratford-upon-Avon. Peter O'Toole played a handsome, heroic, dignified Shylock, juxtaposed against a "gushing, nervous, trivial band of Christians." Some went very far in this direction, like Ellis Robb's production in 1973 at Lincoln Center, where Belmont was a luxury yacht and the guests bored jetsetlers. Notice how decisions about setting, costumes, and music, let alone actors' movements and voice, offer striking, often bold, interpretations of the play's nuances. Trevor Nunn's 1999 film version emphasizes the importance of music, showing Jessica and Shylock sharing a traditional Jewish song in a close, loving duet; then the very last moment in the film has Jessica crying in the foreground, sinking to the floor, and singing that song again.

What confuses audiences and readers is that the play is not a fairy tale. There is a gritty realism and a lack of the whimsical, magical elements that you might find in some of Shakespeare's other comedies. Shylock is not clearly, simply bad, nor are Antonio and his friends clearly, simply good. The relationships that do work out are unsteady, with Bassanio and Gratiano breaking the promise of the rings, Bassanio choosing Antonio over Portia in the trial scene, and Jessica being applauded for converting to Christianity, though she is still somehow an outsider in Belmont. Part of truly appreciating Shakespeare and what he is saying about life, is holding opposing views and feelings at once, accepting conflicting theories about the play, accepting conflicting tones to it, and embracing the ambiguities within characters and their relationships.

Chronology

1564 William Shakespeare is born on April 23 in Stratford-upon-Avon, England

1578–1582 Span of Shakespeare's "Lost Years," covering the time between leaving school and marrying Anne Hathaway of Stratford

1582 At age eighteen Shakespeare marries Anne Hathaway, age twenty-six, on November 28

1583 Susanna Shakespeare, William and Anne's first child, is born in May, six months after the wedding

1584 Birth of twins Hamnet and Judith Shakespeare

1585–1592 Shakespeare leaves his family in Stratford to become an actor and playwright in a London theater company

1587 Public beheading of Mary Queen of Scots

1593–94 The Bubonic (Black) Plague closes theaters in London

1594–96 As a leading playwright, Shakespeare creates some of his most popular work, including *A Midsummer Night's Dream* and *Romeo and Juliet*

1596 Hamnet Shakespeare dies in August at age eleven, possibly of plague

1596–97   *The Merchant of Venice* and *Henry IV, Part One* most likely are written

1599   The Globe Theater opens

1600   *Julius Caesar* is first performed at the Globe

1600–01   *Hamlet* is believed to have been written

1601–02   *Twelfth Night* is probably composed

1603   Queen Elizabeth dies; Scottish king James VI succeeds her and becomes England's James I

1604   Shakespeare pens *Othello*

1605   *Macbeth* is composed

1608–1610   London's theaters are forced to close when the plague returns and kills an estimated 33,000 people

1611   *The Tempest* is written

1613   The Globe Theater is destroyed by fire

1614   Reopening of the Globe

1616   Shakespeare dies on April 23

1623   Anne Hathaway, Shakespeare's widow, dies; a collection of Shakespeare's plays, known as the First Folio, is published

Source Notes

p. 39, textbox, "problematical," Epstein, Norrie. *The Friendly Shakespeare: A Thoroughly Painless Guide to the Best of the Bard,* 239-240.

p. 40, par. 1, "romantic partner," McEvoy, Sean. *Shakespeare, The Basics,* 126.

p. 40, par.2, "secret of life," Goddard, Harold. "Portia Fails the Test for Inner Gold,"100.

p. 68, par. 2, "buried and gone," Goddard, Harold. *The Meaning of Shakespeare Vol 1,* 96.

p. 90, par. 1, "male power," McEvoy, 146.

p. 91, par. 1, "golden casket," Goddard, *The Meaning of Shakespeare Vol 1,* 112.

p. 92, par. 2, "in a different form," Ibid, 88-90.

p. 93, par. 2, "ultimate risk," Epstein, 103.

p. 93, par. 3, "melancholy," Goddard, p. 92.

p. 93, par. 4, "heightened," Epstein, p. 103.

p. 94, par. 2, "end of the play," Ibid, 106-7.

p. 95, par. 1, "another person," Bernthal, Craig. *The Trial of Man; Christianity and judgment in the World of Shakespeare,* p. 94.

p. 95, par. 3, "lead casket," Goddard, *The Meaning of Shakespeare Vol 1,* 96-101.

p. 100, textbox, "not money," Epstein, 107.

p. 101, par. 1, "complexities," Turner, Frederick. *Shakespeare's Twenty-First Century Economics: The Morality of Love and Money,* 55-63.

p. 103, textbox, "of ourselves," Goddard, *The Meaning of Shakespeare Vol 1,* 85.

p. 106, par. 4, "fairy tales," Holland, Norman M. "Two Contrasting Worlds in *The Merchant of Venice*" (in Swisher ed.) p. 120.

p. 107, par. 3, "medium as verse," Halliday, F.E. "Poetry and Prose in *The Merchant of Venice*" (in Swisher ed.) 147.

p. 108, textbox, "beyond reproach," Ibid, p. 155.

p. 109, par. 1, "meaningless chatter," Ibid, p. 84.

p. 109, par. 2, "casket riddles," Hibbard, G.R. "The Language of Argument in *The Merchant of Venice*" (in Swisher ed.) 155.

p. 110, par. 1, "quite impossible," Ibid, p. 162.

p. 111, par. 2, "Barbara Kiefer Lewalski," Ibid, 112.

p. 111, par. 3, "literal interpretation," Ibid, p.87.

p. 112, par. 2, "symbolically," Ibid, p. 126.

p. 113, par. 1, "band of Christians," Gross, John. *Shylock, A Legend and Its Legacy,* p. 327.

A Shakespeare Glossary

The student should not try to memorize these, but only refer to them as needed. We can never stress enough that the best way to learn Shakespeare's language is simply to *hear* it—to hear it spoken well by good actors. After all, small children master every language on earth through their ears, without studying dictionaries, and we should master Shakespeare, as much as possible, the same way.

addition — a name or title (knight, duke, duchess, king, etc.)
admire — to marvel
affect — to like or love; to be attracted to
an — if ("An I tell you that, I'll be hanged.")
approve — to prove or confirm
attend — to pay attention
belike — probably
beseech — to beg or request
betimes — soon; early
bondman — a slave
bootless — futile; useless; in vain
broil — a battle
charge — expense; responsibility; to command or accuse
clepe, clept — to name; named
common — of the common people; below the nobility
conceit — imagination
condition — social rank; quality
countenance — face; appearance; favor
cousin — a relative
cry you mercy — beg your pardon
curious — careful; attentive to detail
dear — expensive
discourse — to converse; conversation
discover — to reveal or uncover
dispatch — to speed or hurry; to send; to kill
doubt — to suspect

entreat — to beg or appeal

envy — to hate or resent; hatred; resentment

ere — before

ever, e'er — always

eyne — eyes

fain — gladly

fare — to eat; to prosper

favor — face, privilege

fellow — a peer or equal

filial — of a child toward its parent

fine — an end; in fine = in sum

fond — foolish

fool — a darling

genius — a good or evil spirit

gentle — well-bred; not common

gentleman — one whose labor was done by servants (Note: to call someone a *gentleman* was not a mere compliment on his manners; it meant that he was above the common people.)

gentles — people of quality

get — to beget (a child)

go to — "go on"; "come off it"

go we — let us go

haply — perhaps

happily — by chance; fortunately

hard by — nearby

heavy — sad or serious

husbandry — thrift; economy

instant — immediate

kind — one's nature; species

knave — a villain; a poor man

lady — a woman of high social rank (Note: *lady* was not a synonym for *woman* or *polite woman*; it was not a compliment, but, like *gentleman*, simply a word referring to one's actual legal status in society.)

leave — permission; "take my leave" = depart (with permission)

lief, lieve — "I had as lief" = I would just as soon; I would rather

like — to please; "it likes me not" = it is disagreeable to me

livery — the uniform of a nobleman's servants; emblem
mark — notice; pay attention
morrow — morning
needs — necessarily
nice — too fussy or fastidious
owe — to own
passing — very
peculiar — individual; exclusive
privy — private; secret
proper — handsome; one's very own ("his proper son")
protest — to insist or declare
quite — completely
require — request
several — different; various
severally — separately
sirrah — a term used to address social inferiors
sooth — truth
state — condition; social rank
still — always; persistently
success — result(s)
surfeit — fullness
touching — concerning; about; as for
translate — to transform
unfold — to disclose
villain — a low or evil person; originally, a peasant
voice — a vote; consent; approval
vouchsafe — to confide or grant
vulgar — common
want — to lack
weeds — clothing
what ho — "hello, there!"
wherefore — why
wit — intelligence; sanity
withal — moreover; nevertheless
without — outside
would — wish

Suggested Essay Topics

1. Does money bring you happiness? Look at how the major characters use and value money. What is Shakespeare telling us about how it affects us or how we should think about it?

2. Women rule! Do the female characters in *The Merchant of Venice* run the show? Are they secretly the real movers and shakers, or do they have to disguise their intelligence and abilities because they are in subservient positions?

3. Watch two film versions of the same scene. Comment on the decisions the directors made to bring out a particular theme (see above for possible themes or motifs on which to focus). Which touches do you like best? Is there anything you would do differently if you were making this film? Make sure to focus on the one theme or motif that you selected.

4. Birds of a feather flock together: Can we judge people by those with whom they spend time? Look at Antonio and his group of friends, or other groupings, such as Portia and Nerissa, or characters who choose to leave one affiliation for another (Jessica leaves Shylock for Lorenzo; Launcelot leaves Shylock for Bassanio; Bassanio chooses Portia, and in a way, leaves Antonio). What does this tell us about the person? Is it fair to judge people this way?

5. True spirituality is rare. Hypocrisy prevails. Is this true in *The Merchant of Venice*? Is this true for us? Are there any characters who adhere to their religions in a respectable and respectful manner? If so, who and why? If not, what are the circumstances or personality flaws that don't allow for this? What is Shakespeare saying about religion?

Testing Your Memory

1. Which two characters' first speeches mention vague sadness?
a) Shylock and Jessica; b) Antonio and Portia; c) Salerio and Solanio;
d) Bassanio and Gratiano.

2. Which character is "the merchant" of the title? a) Shylock; b) Bassanio;
c) Launcelot; d) Antonio.

3. Which casket does the prince of Morocco choose? a) gold; b) silver;
c) lead; d) none; Portia sends him away early.

4. How much money does Shylock lend in the bond with Antonio? a) 500
ducats; b) 1,000 ducats; c) 3,000 ducats; d) 6,000 ducats.

5. Which "master" does Launcelot want to leave? a) Antonio; b) Bassanio;
c) Shylock; d) Gratiano.

6. Shylock asks that Jessica respond to the masque in which way? a) Shut
all doors and windows and ignore the music and noise; b) Join in the fun,
but be careful; c) Enjoy the music, but don't go outside; d) Accompany him
to the party.

7. When Jessica escapes with Lorenzo, how is she dressed? a) like a
princess; b) like a boy; c) in her regular clothes; d) in a costume for the
masque.

8. What does the prince of Arragon get from his choice of caskets?
a) a flower; b) nothing; c) a picture of Portia; d) a fool's head.

9. Which character says, in a famous speech, "If you prick us, do we not
bleed? If you tickle us, do we not laugh? If you poison us, do we not die?
And if you wrong us, shall we not revenge?" a) Antonio; b) the duke;
c) Bassanio; d) Shylock.

10. Jessica traded the ring from her mother for what? a) a dress; b) wine and lodging; c) a monkey; d) passage on a ship.

11. What news does Bassanio receive just after winning Portia's hand? a) Antonio cannot repay Shylock; b) Antonio will come visit him in Belmont; c) Launcelot would like to be his servant; d) Jessica has run away with Lorenzo.

12. Where does Portia say she and Nerissa will wait for their new husbands while they take care of the business with Shylock and Antonio? a) at home in Belmont; b) in a nearby country home; c) in Venice; d) at a monastery.

13. When Shylock is asked to back down from his pursuit of the bond, his response is: a) I will if you pay me three times the original amount; b) You could pay me more than six times the amount, and I still wouldn't back down; c) If only Antonio would apologize, I'd end this; d) Bring back my daughter, and then we can talk.

14. Which character says this in a famous speech? "The quality of mercy is not strained, / It droppeth as the gentle rain from heaven / Upon the place beneath." a) Portia; b) Antonio; c) the duke; d) Shylock.

15. What trick does Portia as the lawyer use to turn the trial around? a) Shylock can't use a knife; b) Shylock must accept twice the original loan instead; c) Shylock may cut, but cannot let Antonio bleed; d) Since Shylock is not a Christian, he has to wait before the bond can be recognized.

16. In what way does Antonio "compromise" with Shylock at the end of the trial? a) He requires that Shylock pay back all interest charged to others, in return for his life; b) He requires that Shylock convert to Christianity, and will the forfeiture due Antonio to Jessica and Lorenzo, but be allowed to live; c) He requires that Shylock leave Venice and never return, but not owe any fine; d) He says that Shylock must stop the usury business and then be free.

17. Portia takes what in payment for her services as a lawyer? a) nothing; b) the three thousand ducats originally owed Shylock; c) a ring from Antonio; d) her own wedding ring from Bassanio.

18. Which character comments on the beauty and power of music in the moonlight? a) Jessica; b) Lorenzo; c) Gratiano; d) Portia.

19. What news does Antonio receive at the end? a) His ships were not lost after all; b) He lost even more of his fortune; c) Shylock is dead; d) Another friend needs a loan.

20. Which two characters are unattached at the end of the play? a) Portia and Nerissa; b) Shylock and Jessica; c) Gratiano and Bassanio; d) Shylock and Antonio.

Answer Key

12. d.; 13. b.; 14. a.; 15. c.; 16. b.; 17. c.; 18. b.; 19. a.; 20. d.

1. b.; 2. d.; 3. c.; 4. c.; 5. c.; 6. a.; 7. b.; 8. c.; 9. d.; 10. d.; 11. a.;

Further Information

BOOKS

Hinds, Gareth. *The Merchant of Venice (Graphic Shakespeare)*. Cambridge, MA: Candlewick Press, 2008.

Middleton, Haydn. *True Lives: Shakespeare*. New York: Oxford University Press, 2009.

Mittelstaedt, Walt. *Understanding Literature: A Student's Guide to William Shakespeare*. Berkeley Heights, NJ: Enslow Publishers, 2005.

WEBSITES

Cummings Study Guides   www.cummingsstudyguides.net

In Search of Shakespeare   www.pbs.org/shakespeare/

Shakespeare Resource Center   www.bardweb.net

FILMS

The Merchant of Venice. Directed by Michael Radford, starring Al Pacino, Joseph Fiennes, and Lynn Collins, 2004.

The Merchant of Venice. Directed by Chris Hunt and Trevor Nunn, a British television production starring Henry Goodman, Alexander Hanson, and Derbhle Crotty, 2001.

AUDIO BOOKS AND RECORDINGS

The Merchant of Venice on CD. Narrators: Haydn Gwynne, Bill Nighy, Arkangel Cast. Published by Audio Partners, Auburn, CA, 2005.

The Merchant of Venice, Stratford Festival on CD. Narrators: Peter Hutt, Donald Carrier. Canadian Broadcasting Company, 2002.

Bibliography

Bernthal, Craig. *The Trial of Man: Christianity and Judgment in the World of Shakespeare*. Wilmington, DE: ISI Books, 2003.

Calderwood, James L. and Harold E. Toliver, eds. *Essays in Shakespearean Criticism*. Englewood Cliffs, NJ: Prentice-Hall Inc., 1970.

Epstein, Norrie. *The Friendly Shakespeare: A Thoroughly Painless Guide to the Best of the Bard*. New York: Viking, A Winokur/Boates Book, 1993.

Goddard, Harold C. *The Meaning of Shakespeare, Vol. 1*. 81–116. Chicago: The University of Chicago Press, 1967.

Goddard, Harold C. "Portia Fails the Test for Inner Gold." In *Readings on "The Merchant of Venice."* Edited by Clarice Swisher. San Diego: Greenhaven Press Inc., 2000.

Gross, John. *Shylock, A Legend and Its Legacy*. New York: Simon and Schuster, 1992.

Halliday, F. E. "Poetry and Prose in *The Merchant of Venice*." In *Readings on "The Merchant of Venice."* Edited by Clarice Swisher. San Diego: Greenhaven Press Inc., 2000.

Hibbard, G. R. "The Language of Argument in *The Merchant of Venice*." In *Readings on "The Merchant of Venice."* Edited by Clarice Swisher. San Diego: Greenhaven Press Inc., 2000.

Holland, Norman M. "Two Contrasting Worlds in *The Merchant of Venice*." In *Readings on "The Merchant of Venice."* Edited by Clarice Swisher. San Diego: Greenhaven Press Inc., 2000.

Kay, Dennis. "The Historical Context of *The Merchant of Venice*." In *Readings on "The Merchant of Venice."* Edited by Clarice Swisher. San Diego: Greenhaven Press Inc., 2000.

McEvoy, Sean. *Shakespeare, The Basics*. London: Routledge and Kegan Paul, 2000.

The Merchant of Venice. Directed by Michael Radford. Sony Pictures Classics, Film Council, Film Fund Luxemburg, 2004.

Turner, Frederick. *Shakespeare's Twenty-First Century Economics: The Morality of Love and Money*. Oxford: Oxford University Press, 1999.

Index

Page numbers in **boldface** are illustrations.

UNITED STATES

SHAKESPEARE
1564 ~ 1964

5c

About the Author

Sara Schupack is from Northern California, and has taught English at many levels, from fourth grade through college. She studied literature at Yale, creative writing at New York University, and teaching at the University of Hong Kong. Most recently she has taught writing at two community colleges. She writes short stories and creative nonfiction. Currently she studies education in a doctoral program. She lives with her son in Western Massachusetts.